GET THE
JOB
YOU WANT IN

DAYS

THE STEP-BY-STEP **ACTION** PLAN
THAT HELPS YOU FIND THE **JOB**
THAT'S **RIGHT** FOR YOU...
AND TELLS **YOU** HOW TO GET IT!

GARY JOSEPH GRAPPO

KOG
PA

D1313074

First published in 1997 by Berkley Books, New York
This edition published in 1998 by Kogan Page Limited

Kogan Page Limited
120 Pentonville Road
London N1 9JN

British Library Cataloguing in Publication Data

A CIP record for this book is available from the British Library.

ISBN 0 7494 2586 5

Typeset by Jo Brereton, Primary Focus, Haslington, Cheshire
Printed and bound in Great Britain by Clays Ltd, St Ives plc

To my parents – who taught me never to say 'I can't'

To my sisters – who helped me to believe 'I can'

To Tim – friend and colleague

And in memory of my brother, James Paul Grappo, Jr,
who recently began to live.

Special Acknowledgements

Leonard Evans
Denis Waitley
Brian Tracy

Contents

Figures and exercises

Introduction

Someone once said, 'Necessity is the mother of invention'. Perhaps someone should also have said, 'Invention is the process by which we increase the quality of life not only for ourselves but also for others'.

Learning to help yourself before taking on the awesome task of helping others is often a difficult lesson. It's the minor lessons in life that often, in time, turn out to be the most profound life-changing principles. Master them and we are compelled to tell the world.

Writing this book results first and foremost from being a job-seeker myself. This system, like most inventions, is the result of personal trial and error. It is also the result of a sincere desire to help others, as I am a professional with many years' experience in the human resource field.

I do not separate my professional from my personal life. The philosophy for both is the law of cause and effect, which can be stated in a variety of ways:

- for every action, there is a reaction;
- whatever you sow, so shall you reap;
- give and it will be given to you.

This book not only makes good business sense, it is also based on very fundamental principles for successful living. It searches for ears that hear and eyes that see. The risk remains, however, that, after all is said and done, it may only be ink on paper. Even so, those of you who thirst for success in all you do will take this book and make it a success in your own lives.

It is important that you read this book from beginning to end. If chapters are read out of sequence, an important building process is thwarted. There are 30 key concepts that depend on the same principles utilized by house builders and brick layers: the foundations must be solid. The full significance of the 30 key concepts will be realized when each previous step is understood, accepted and acted on. The first two chapters are particularly essential to the building process as they are not only the foundations of it but also its roots.

After reading the book in its entirety, I urge you to make daily use of the activity planner. Besides giving you an action plan, it also contains a quick reference for the 30 key concepts. This is provided to help you reduce pages of information to key essentials, and these concepts should be memorized and acted on. With these tools, nothing can stop you!

1
Goal-setting preliminaries

Just out of college, I had the fortunate experience – which I will share in more detail later – of meeting an elderly pastor, a noted author and speaker by the name of Leonard Evans. It was he who helped me get my career off to the right start. Leonard had a way of looking you in the eye and pointedly asking the right questions. He never gave advice. His technique was to make you create your own solutions.

When I went to him seeking counsel about my career, the first questions he asked revolved around goal-setting. 'What are your goals? What do you like to do?' he asked. The questions left me speechless. I must admit, I was taken by surprise. I had never thought about those things before. At that point, I had very little to say.

Leonard then provoked a reaction with his next question. 'If you could do anything you wanted – forget about money, opportunity, or the right connections –what would you be doing with your life right now?' Immediately, a lengthy discussion transpired. For the first time in my life, I was forced to clearly identify, verbalize and write down my likes and dislikes. Through this question, the lightbulbs began to go on. The message was clear: go after the things you like to do and the money will follow. There is a book that has been very successful and summarizes where Reverend Evans was leading me. The title is *Do What You Love, the Money Will Follow,* by Marsha Sinetar.

An illustration of this is the story of a great pioneer woman. As a child, she asked her parents for a set of paints and brushes. Her interest in painting was dismissed as costly and foolish. Later, as a young teenager, she was married off to an older gentleman, and she raised a large family. Only when she was a 75-year-old widow did she decide to do what she had always loved: paint. Within five years, she established American primitive art as a style. She became known as Grandma Moses. After an exhibition at the Metropolitan Museum of Art and others around the USA, some of her works began to sell for over £60,000 each. The sale of one painting yielded her more money in a day than she and her husband had made in a lifetime.

Brian Tracy, in his tape series *The Science of Self-confidence*, states that there are four possible paths for a person's life. They are:

1   things that are hard to do to and hard to learn, such as restoring classic cars;
2   things that are easy to learn but hard to do, such as carrying bricks to and fro on a building site;
3   things that are hard to learn but easy to do, such as operating a modern till;
4   things that are easy to learn and easy to do, which varies from person to person.

Brian Tracy explains that the fourth path is what we ideally should be doing with our lives. These things that are so easy for us may be hard to learn and hard to do for others. Reflect a moment on the things that you learn easily and perform well. They are generally the very things that make you happy because you enjoy doing them. This type of introspection begins to uncover your ideal career path and goals.

Before beginning your job search, it is important to identify your strengths, likes, weaknesses and dislikes. Based on this information, you will have identified that which produces an almost religious fervour inside of you, propelling your career towards success.

Before establishing goals, it is important to realize how they are achieved. After all, no one wants to set a goal that is impossible to achieve. In fact, it is the fear of failure that discourages many people from setting goals. These people assume that they will never fail if they never set goals. This is far from the truth. What is worse than failure? Never trying! Making no goals and no decisions is true failure. Otherwise, there are no failures in life, just learning experiences.

When properly motivated, we can attain our goals. As a child, you may remember being promised an ice-cream or a toy if you would behave and not embarrass everyone on a family outing. This motivational reward system certainly had its merits. It's also good psychology, according to Pavlov and his experiments with dogs. Think about what motivates you. What propels you to achieve your goals?

Many times over the years I have asked the students who have attended my seminars what motivates them. They consistently give four responses:

1 money;
2 security;
3 self-respect;
4 recognition.

I believe this list accurately represents those things that motivate all of us in life. The job search process can be difficult. It can be downright gruelling at times. People tend not to be motivated in the face of rejection. However, daily recognition of what motivates you will keep your attitude healthy and in perspective. I suggest you write down your motivators on a small piece of paper. Place them in your wallet or purse and review them when you need an extra push to keep you going. Surely this is one good way to maintain a positive attitude. In the next chapter we will discuss other ways.

Take a moment to do the goal-setting exercises that follow. You will discover much about yourself and begin to formulate exactly what it is that makes you happy and will also make you money.

When you have completed the following exercises, you will discover some simple methods to help you draw conclusions from your answers and create personal goal strategies.

Identifying likes and dislikes

List all the things you generally like and dislike. This is a brainstorming session, so there are no right or wrong answers. Also, keep in mind that no answer is too trite – all responses are valid.

Likes	Dislikes
Example: Working with and for people.	*Example:* Numbers, details and deskwork.

Identifying strengths and weaknesses

List what you believe to be your strengths and weaknesses. Again, this is a brainstorming session, so there are no right or wrong answers. Also, as with the last exercise, keep in mind that no answer it too trite – all responses are valid.

Strengths	Weaknesses
Example: Good telephone voice. Effective use of the telephone in a business setting.	*Example:* Financial reports and spreadsheets.

Fundamental goal-setting questions and answers

Answer the following questions openly and honestly. This is not a time to colour the facts. In this exercise, as well, there are no right or wrong answers.

Questions	Answers
1 What sort of salary are you looking for?	
2 Under what circumstances would you be willing to take less? How much less?	
3 If you were offered a job that guaranteed you complete job and career happiness but paid much less, would you take it?	
4 Where do you want to be in your career one year from now?	
5 Where do you want to be in your career five years from now?	
6 What motivates you to be successful with your life and career?	
7 What personal obstacles are you aware of that may keep you from achieving your goals?	
8 Are you willing to take action to remove these obstacles?	
9 What actions are necessary, in your opinion?	

First, let's take a look at your likes and dislikes. By focusing on your preferences, you can begin to determine what kind of job would make you happy. As discussed earlier, the things that make you happy also make you money. Your dislikes reveal what you should consider ruling out as a major career focus. Unfortunately, some of your dislikes will come along with any career, no matter how compatible the job is with your likes.

Let's say, for instance, that the first example under likes and dislikes on page 6 was written by you. You've stated that you like working with and for people. This realization is important. You should apply for jobs that involve interaction with people. Rule out a cloistered position in a two-room office, preparing reports – it's not you. Sounds obvious, but often people take jobs that they are dissatisfied with after only a few months. The reason they feel frustrated is that the work is fundamentally opposite to their basic likes.

Take a look at your strengths and weaknesses. Let's say the first example on page 7 was written by you. You have stated that you have a good phone voice and know how to use the telephone effectively in business. Begin to brainstorm by writing a list of jobs (such as airline reservations, telesales sales and customer service positions) that would fit that description. Don't stop until you list at least ten careers for each strength.

After you have made your list, review the answers you gave to goal-setting questions on page 8. Now, on a plain sheet of paper, write a master list of 25 job opportunities (be as specific as possible) that fit with the answers to these questions and play on your likes and strengths. Do not stop writing until you have listed all 25 opportunities.

Ultimately, the purpose of goal-setting is to eliminate concerns and worries. Do you worry about your future? Replace worry with clear direction combined with action. People who worry can always think of reasons for not taking action to improve their situation. Excuses, though, simply prolong the pain and retard the ability to find a solution. Denis Waitley states in his book, *The Psychology of Winning*, 'Losers do what is quick and easy' whereas winners 'do what is difficult and necessary.' I hope you have made a commitment to live by the winners' formula.

With this in mind, when you have completed the exercises in this chapter, you are then ready to begin the quest for the right career.

2
Start with a positive attitude

Getting the job you want depends more on how you think than on something you do. According to Dr Denis Waitley, author of *The Psychology of Winning*, a positive attitude is the single most important asset to achieving goals in life and being respected by others as a winner. Dr Waitley states, 'Before any Super Bowl team has won and long before an Olympic athlete takes the gold, each has visualized and believed that they are a winner.'

The mind is the beginning of the reality you create for yourself. Each day you programme your mind much like a computer programmer sets up a computer. There is a computer term that you may be familiar with – GIGO, which stands for garbage in, garbage out! What are you programming your mind with?

**If you think you can't, you won't,
but if you think you can, you will!**

We speak to ourselves and create our own programming at a rate of over 1,000 words per minute. This is what is meant by 'self-talk'. Some things that happen to us – like the weather – are out of our control. But, for the most part, reality is a direct result of your beliefs and what you say to yourself. For instance, if someone believes consciously or unconsciously that he is 'never going to be promoted', or that she will 'never be good enough at computers to get a better job', then that person will act out those beliefs in their mind with negative internal chatter, or, self-talk. The resulting actions or, should I say, inaction, make their negative beliefs come true.

2

Practise positive self-talk:
'I can! I will! I know I can do it!'

As you begin your 30-day success plan, I have a very important question to ask you. What is your self-talk? What do you say to yourself when you lie in bed ready to fall asleep at night? What do you say to yourself when you wake up in the morning and contemplate a new day of activities? What are you thinking during your waking hours or daydreaming about over a cup of coffee? Be honest!

A winner's positive self-talk will sound something like this:

'I know I can do it!'

'I have the drive, spirit and stamina to be successful!'

'I always achieve what I set my mind to do!'

'I'm the best and I know others respect and like me as well!'

'I like myself!'

'I take full responsibility for myself and nothing can stop me from achieving my goals!'

Best-selling author and behavioural researcher Dr Shad Helmstetter has conducted extensive research in the area of self-talk. He states, 'I have received thousands of letters from people who, in the middle of their adulthood, realized that they had believed something about themselves all their lives that was totally false.' 'One man in particular', he remembers, 'had never finished senior school.' His parents often said to others that their son 'was not as smart as his sisters.' Another man, an alcoholic, had been told repeatedly while growing up that he, 'was just like his father,' who also was an alcoholic. Here is a list of many untruths, the negative self-talk people entertain about themselves every day.

Fifty destructive affirmations

The following is a sample list of 50 of the most frequently used phrases many of us say to ourselves that, in the end, sabotage our own quest for success. Place a tick in the box next to the phrases you have said to yourself, either seriously or in jest.

I can't remember names. ☐

It's going to be another one of those days. ☐

It's just no use! ☐

I just know it won't work. ☐

Nothing ever goes right for me. ☐

That's just my luck. ☐

I'm so clumsy. ☐

I don't have the talent. ☐

I've never been good at that. ☐

I'm just not creative. ☐

Everything I eat goes straight to my hips. ☐

I've tried everything, nothing works. ☐

I can't seem to get organized. ☐

Today just isn't my day. ☐

I can never afford the things I want. ☐

I already know I won't like it. ☐

Why even try, I know already it won't work. ☐

No matter what I do, I can't seem to lose the weight. ☐

I never have enough time. ☐

I just don't have the patience for that. ☐

That really makes me angry. ☐

It's another typical Monday. □

When will I ever learn? □

It won't work, face it. □

I feel ill just thinking about it. □

Sometimes I just hate myself. □

I'm just no good. □

I'm too shy. □

I never command any respect. □

I never know what to say. □

With my luck, I'll trip and fall. □

With my luck I don't have a chance. □

I'd like to stop smoking, but I can't seem to quit. □

Things just aren't working out for me right now. □

I don't have the energy I used to. □

I'm really out of shape. □

I never have any money left over at the end of the month. □

Why should I try – it's not going to work anyway. □

I've never been any good at that. □

I'll never be promoted. □

My desk is always a mess. □

I always lose things. □

I can never find anything. □

The only kind of luck I have is bad luck. □

I never win anything. □

I always lose. □

I feel like I'm over the hill. □

Someone always beats me to it. □

Nobody likes me. □

I'll never find a good job. □

Source: Dr Shad Helmstetter, *What to Say When You Talk to Yourself.*

Well, how did you do? Don't feel bad if you ticked many of the phrases in the above exercise. However, even if your self-talk sounds like the list above, it's never too late to join the team of winners in life. You can take action and break old habits of self-talk. Utilize the following simple, but life-changing, principle that can make you a winner, too!

3

Neutralize negative self-talk ('I'll never find a good job') with positive, winning statements

Change your negative programming with opposite, positive statements. Whether at home or driving in your car, speak to yourself out loud or, if others are around, in your mind. Make statements such as:

'I like myself!'

'I know the interviewer will like me, too!'

'I am qualified for the job.'

'I am the best at what I do.'

'They will hire me.'

'There is no such thing as luck.'

'I always achieve what I set out to do.'

Also, speak to yourself with simple, positive statements, such as, 'I can.'

I'd now like to tell you about my own experience to illustrate the role the power of the mind plays in each of our successes. Just like many of you reading this book, I was in the job market some years ago, right after I graduated from college. With no job offer waiting for me, I decided to return home for the summer. Determined, I began sending out CVs in response to advertisements for jobs all over the country. After two months, I was feeling frustrated as I had had few responses for all my efforts.

Then I met Leonard Evans, an older gentleman who was pastor of a large congregation. I knew of his reputation as a wise confidant. I also knew he was well connected with wealthy businessmen in the area. I called him to ask if we could meet for lunch and he accepted.

At an Oriental restaurant, over *moo goo gai pan*, his favourite dish, Leonard Evans listened to a young man communicate his hopes, dreams, frustrations and inability to find himself. I was doing all the talking. I thought that if I sounded in a bad enough way, he would just call one of his business contacts and tell them to give me a job. That was not the case. However, what he did tell me, when I finally shut up, was more valuable than a job.

Somewhere between the main course and the fortune cookies, Leonard asked, 'Gary, have you ever read the story *Acres of Diamonds*?' 'No,' I replied, but I thought to myself, *'The last thing I need is another book to read after five years of college.'* He continued, 'It is a true story written around the turn of the century. I suggest you read it, but I'll briefly tell you the story now.

'There was a man and his family who lived on a farm in the middle of the desert. The man's family had lived there for many generations. He was tired of the problems of irrigation and the poverty that came with being a tiller of the land.

'One day he decided to take his family and search the world for more money and a better life. But first, he had to sell the farm, and that he did for a pittance. After years of travel throughout Europe, he was no better off and still searching.

'Then the news came that devastated his soul. A message arrived by telegram that the family he sold his farm to had discovered acres of diamonds and found good fortune in their own back yard!'

Leonard looked at me with peaceful confidence and said, 'You've been working hard, looking everywhere to find a job and, more importantly, to find your purpose in life. What I am suggesting to you through this story is that your success is first in your own mind. Your mind is your own back yard. Believe in yourself and you can bring about success, no matter where you live, no matter where you are and no matter what circumstances life gives you.'

That was the most important lunch I have had, or will ever have. Not many weeks later, I found a job in my own town, despite 12 per cent unemployment! More importantly, that day I discovered a universal truth that has kept my life successful ever since.

I hope you will go to the library and read *Acres of Diamonds*. Realize its truth: quit fighting, stop struggling, look inside yourself – analyse your strengths, identify your skills and be positive about where you are in life. Your acres of diamonds are in your own back yard.

═══ 4 ═══

Don't blame others –
take responsibility for yourself
and your career

Avoid blaming previous jobs, bosses, family or even your parents for your current situation. As long as you make excuses for your current situation in life, you will never take active, personal responsibility for yourself, you'll always rely on someone or something else to make you successful. That only works for Cinderella! In real life, *you* have to make it happen.

Winners realize that adverse circumstances are a fact of life. Voltaire, the great French writer, likened life to being dealt a hand of cards. What you do with the cards determines your success.

Some people dwell on negative aspects of their past, when they were a child or a teenager. Over and over, they bitterly recount the same parental incidents that explain why they are so miserable today. I hope you avoid this pitfall. Admit the past, but don't let it control you. The past cannot be changed. Circumstances cannot be changed. You cannot control external situations. You can control your reaction to them, however, and take clear, precise and positive action. Essentially, anyone can make lemonade out of lemons.

5

Practise visualization when you are lying awake in the morning or evening, seeing yourself already working at and enjoying the career you want

Visualization is the key step to creating and reinforcing a positive attitude. When you lie awake in the morning or evening, visualize already working at and enjoying the career you want.

Many people wonder what is meant by the term visualization. It is not necessary to see images. Some people simply say positive affirmations in their minds, in a way that is similar to the self-talk of winners described earlier. Other people prefer to picture themselves occupied in successful activities. Whichever technique you choose, you must set aside a quiet time every day for visualization.

With visualization, you can take positive action to assure a positive attitude. See yourself working successfully at your ideal job or replay successful events from your past in your mind. Write ten personal positive affirmations you will use in your visualization time. Here are some examples.

Each day I get better and better.

I have everything I need inside of me to become successful.

I am a dynamic and well-liked person.

I feel healthy.

I am happy.

I know I can do it.

You can literally create hundreds more affirmations and visualizations, but, below, write down just ten that are relevant to you.

Ten personal positive affirmations

1 _____

2 _____

3 _____

4 _____

5 _____

6 _____

7 _____

8 _____

9 _____

10 _____

Every day you should use the ten affirmations you have just written down. Add to them often, and find quality quiet time to visualize them.

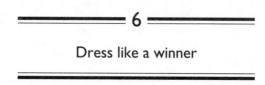

6

Dress like a winner

A successful person in life not only thinks like a winner, they dress like a winner. Make sure your clothes are clean and pressed and your hair and nails are clean and your image is professional and simple.

According to research, verbal content comprises only 7 per cent of your total message. Your visual image comprises 93 per cent of the message you convey to others. What you say is only a small percentage of what others perceive you to be. Indeed, according to Janet Elsea's book, *The Four-minute Sell*, an interview is decided within the first four minutes based on image. Others would argue that it is actually 30 seconds or less.

A negative first impression may make it difficult or impossible to sell to, influence or persuade someone. Think of a recent time when you attended a party or family gathering and met someone new. Did they make a positive or negative first impression on you? If it was positive, how so? If it was negative, what turned you off? Was it their mannerisms, hair, clothes, jewellery, perfume or aftershave? Remember, you never get a second chance to make a good first impression.

I remember the time I had to interview a number of people for an on-site computer trainer job. All day long, the applicants drifted in for their appointment times. The secretary had each wait in the reception area. Nothing out of the ordinary happened until a young lady arrived dressed as for an Easter Sunday church service – wearing a large yellow-rimmed hat, yellow shoes and a yellow and orange dress. The outfit was beautiful, but it stuck out like a sore thumb in a business environment. It stuck out so much that the other employees were still talking about this job-seeker a year later. The other six people who were interviewed were long forgotten.

In business, you want to draw attention to your skills, not your looks. When you leave an interview, you want the interviewer to remember you, not something you were wearing.

You can control your image so as to suit the company intending to interview you. If you believe it is in your best interest to look older, then dress more conservatively. Wear quality accessories. Should you feel it is in your best interest to look younger, style your hair in a more fashionable way and wear slightly more up-to-date clothes. Your image can influence others in any direction you wish to take them.

Create the appropriate image for the company and industry you would like to enter. If you don't want to, are you sabotaging yourself by not dressing the part? When necessary, wear a conservative suit or casual clothes. Those who have successful interviews are those who have also mastered the art of creating the correct image for a given situation. Avoid getting locked into one look for all interviews. Put some thought into what the company is like and the style associated with the position you are being interviewed for, then dress accordingly. Whatever the case may be, the fact remains: image sells!

Research shows that the two most important visual cues – the parts an interviewer looks at during an interview – are an interviewee's hair and shoes. They start at the top and go directly to the bottom. 'Which means, in theory, you could arrive naked as long as you have well-combed hair and shiny shoes. However, this is only a theory, and is not recommended,' Camille Lavington, a career specialist at a division of the Sara-Lee Corporation, says jokingly.

The components of image

Just for the record, when we discuss image and the impact it has on an interviewer in the first 30 seconds, the main components we mean by this are:

- hair;
- shoes;
- clothing;
- hands;
- fingernails;
- skin;
- hygiene;
- perfume or aftershave;
- make-up;
- jewellery;
- teeth;
- facial expressions;
- body language;
- accessories;
- voice tone/pitch/quality;
- manners/politeness/etiquette.

Take action regarding your image. Stop a moment and take stock of your professional wardrobe and accessories by doing the following exercise. If you tick off items that need to be replaced, consider borrowing those items from a friend or family member. You will save money and accomplish the same result.

Professional wardrobe checklist			
Item	Have	Don't have	Needs replacing
1 Interview suit			
2 Alternative suit			
3 Shirt/blouse			
4 Polished shoes			
5 Tie (men)			
6 Attractive watch			
7 Black notebook			
8 Smart pen			
9 Other accessories:			
_____			
_____			
_____			

A common misconception about image is the notion that you need to make an individuality statement when appearing in public. Save the trendy jewellery, shaved head and pierced nose and so on for parties and weekends. If you want career success, then dress the part at all business-related activities. This even includes after-hours business-related parties and dinners. Trendy dressing is better for your career when it is kept for parties among family and friends.

Let's review now what we've learned in this chapter:

- If you think you can't, you won't.
- Practise positive self-talk.
- Neutralize negative self-talk with positive statements.
- Take responsibility for your own life.
- Practise visualization.
- Dress like a winner.

3
Prepare a successful CV and covering letter

A common misconception most job-seekers have is that those re-cruiting new staff have plenty of time to read CVs. For more than five years I have been personally acquainted with many of the personnel and human resources managers of leading companies. They would agree that their job is much more complicated than reading CVs and hiring employees. Like all business profession-als, they have meetings, need to travel and perform other tasks related to their job. Essentially, they are very busy people.

7

Design a one-page CV, giving just enough information to prompt an interview – leave the reader wanting more

As we have seen, whoever will be reading your CV will not have all the time in the world, so use the KISS principle, which means Keep It Simple, Salesperson! You are, after all, selling yourself! As with most things in life, the most convincing and the most profound concepts are those that are stated in the simplest terms. The fast-paced business world of personnel and other managers, overwhelmed by travel, fax machines, deadlines and computers, demands a one-page CV, which can be reviewed quickly. When you create an informative, one-page CV, you have achieved two important factors in your favour:

- your one-page CV saves its reader valuable time and so it is more likely that it will be read.
- you have given its reader just enough information to prompt them to call you for interview so they can find out more.

Do this and you'll be getting more phone calls than your competition.

Often, job-seekers attending my seminars discuss with me their objections to a one-page CV. The most common one I hear is, 'Yes, but you just don't seem to understand. I've had all these years of experience and, in so many words, I'm so great and wonderful, it can't possibly all fit on one page!' My response to this objection is, in the words of Brian Tracy, author of *The Psychology of Success,* 'Well, go try it 20 times. If it still doesn't work, call and tell me, then go back and do it your way.'

Stick to the formula – it works! Don't try to tell your whole story on paper. Leave the reader wanting more. Don't feel obliged to list every day of every year since you began working. If you have been working for a few years, omit months in your chronology of dates, just listing the years. It's easier to read. Only include the experience relevant to the job for which you are applying. If you have just left school or graduated, list your education near the beginning of the CV. If you have been employed for a few years, list your education near the end. Your work history, what you have accomplished, is more important.

In the hi-tech age of personal computers, desktop publishing, spell check facilities and laser printers, there is no excuse for a scruffy CV. Your competition is making use of technology and so should you. A program like Word should be used to produce your CV. In Word, for example, the user is provided with three CV template options: Contemporary, Elegant and Professional, plus access to more templates and wizards and the CV Wizard. To reach them, click on 'File', then 'New' and click on 'Other Documents'.

Complete the template of your choice with your particular data. It's that simple. Next, print it out on a laser printer. The result is a spectacular-looking and professional CV.

8

Print out your CV on white paper only, using a professional computer software template, use spell check facility and make sure that your grammar is correct

---

Unless you are looking for a position in advertising, art or design, steer clear of colourful and trendy CVs. Often people choose colourful paper for their CVs because they think that colour increases the chances of its standing out. However, you run the risk that whoever reads your CV will not like that colour, will think the CV looks trendy and that the writer is immature. It's better to have your CV look too conservative than to risk it looking too flashy. The bottom line is that white is always appropriate. However, one way to achieve an element of difference in a positive way is to use high-quality paper, such as high white laid, which has a textured surface and is thicker than, say, photocopying paper. Go to your local print shop and browse through what will surely be an excellent selection of fine papers.

There are other pitfalls and traps that CV writers fall into unknowingly. Beware! Here are my top ten CV-writing pitfalls to avoid.

The top ten CV-writing pitfalls to avoid

1 Too long.

2 Scattered. The information does not flow. Hard to follow.

3 Big sentences, big paragraphs, too much that says too little.

4 Small type (never go smaller than 12 point) and poor-quality printer.

5 Sparse. Looks like you never did anything in your last job(s).

6 Few white spaces.

7 Listing of height, weight, marital status, sex, health. Who cares?

8 The spell check did not catch everything, that is, 'there's' instead of 'theirs', other typographical errors and poor grammar.

9 Too many typefaces, too fancy, too busy, resulting in it being too distracting!

10 Lacking a target. It arrives on someone's desk but does not clearly focus on their need. It lacks target language.

Now that you are convinced that a one-page CV is in your best interest, I've got good news for you; there is a time and a place for an 'expanded' two- or three-page CV. Briefly, here's how it works. The one-page CV is used for cold leads. For instance, a newspaper ad would be considered a cold lead. Send a one-page CV to companies that you have no personal contact with or when no personal referral from a friend has been given to help get your foot in the door.

The 'expanded' two- or three-page CV is used for warm leads. For instance, if a family member asks you to contact a hiring manager friend, that is a warm lead. Send your two- or three-page CV to people and companies that you are personally referred to, and you know will give you personalized attention. Also, the expanded CV makes a great 'leave behind' at the close of a first interview that has resulted from sending in your one-page CV.

Below is Gregory Miller's two-page CV that he uses for warm leads. Directly following it is the edited one-page CV version, which he uses for cold leads. His CV is an excellent example to follow for anyone who is not a recent graduate and has been in their career for some time. Stephanie Chambers' CV follows Gregory Miller's. Her young career and limited work history make the CV naturally a one-page one. It is an excellent example of how to set out a CV if you have just left school or graduated and are beginning to embark on a career. Use these examples as the basis for your own CVs, inserting your information.

Sample expanded two-page CV

Gregory E. Miller
23 Hawthorn Gardens
London W11 2ZA
0171-623 45678
gem@aol.com

Summary of qualifications

- Over ten years' experience in audio visual production management.
- Extensive experience in numerous electronics training courses in design and facilitation.
- Comprehensive knowledge of computers, software and networks.
- Extensive experience in new facility electronic systems design and implementation.
- Good, written and oral communication skills.

Work Experience

- **1993–present**   **ABC Productions, London**
  Position: Manager Audio Visual Production
  Managed audio visual technology for a large, state-of-the-art conference centre. Oversaw final stages of the facility's construction and equipment installation.
  Recruited, trained and managed a staff of 12. Upgraded the centre's technical equipment needs, as a result of changing requirements. Responsible for the maintenance and repair of all equipment. Clients delighted with completed project.

- **1992–1993**   **ABC Productions, London**
  Position: Instructor
  Responsible for the instruction of over 100 A-level Electronics students.
  Designed customized curriculums and selected appropriate textbooks. Personally developed laboratory experiments, specified and ordered lab materials and conducted all classes.

- **1991–1992**   **Sound Systems, Glasgow**
  Position: Independent Contractor
  Conducted a needs assessment of the client's multimedia
  theatre. Designed and prototyped all circuitry, conducted tests,
  designed circuit boards and installed a substantial and intricate
  theatre system. Wrote and produced documentation for the
  system.

- **1990–1991**   **ABC Productions,**
  London
  Position: Independent Contractor
  Developed theatrical electrical systems for a cinema.
  Specified acoustics, seating, layout and the relevant
  architectural features.
  Coordinated efforts with the cinema's physical plant, architect,
  vendors and subcontractors. Conducted an initial on-site needs
  assessment.
  Generated written specifications and detailed construction
  drawings.
  Installed projection, audio and theatrical lighting systems.

- **1986–1990**   **Newstime, London**
  Position: Electronic Systems Manager
  Designed, specified, installed and repaired all electronic
  systems, including telephone and satellite reception technology
  for this news network.
  Developed and constructed a PC-based digital control system
  for the automated operation of all network audio feeds.
  Communicated with engineers at affiliate stations regarding all
  technical matters.

Education
- BA Electronics, University of Leeds
- Certificate in Educaton

Awards and Achievements
- Member, BECTU
- Member, Amalgamated Engineering and Electrical Union

References
- Available on request

Before we take a look at Gregory Miller's *one* -page CV, let us take a moment to recognize why his two-page format is reader-friendly.

Enhancing readability

Enhance your CV's readability by using the following.

- <u>Bold</u> Notice how it draws your eyes to key sections.

- <u>Bullets</u> Surveys have shown that almost 75 per cent of personnel and other managers prefer reading a CV with points set out as bulleted lists.

- <u>Indentations</u> Creates lots of white, open spaces, which are more inviting than text of uniform width, closely packed together.

- <u>Large headlines</u> These draw your eyes to key sections.

- <u>Summary of qualifications</u> This is a list of a few hot selling features about you that make the reader want to learn more. Use this part of your CV to address every requirement given in an advertisement. This works on the same principle as do headlines in a newspaper.

- <u>Awards and achievements</u> Everyone has them! Take some time and come up with a few. Without this section you appear average!

OK, now that you know why Gregory Miller's CV is effective, notice how in the next example it has been ruthlessly edited (but necessarily) to just key points, resulting in a one-page document. Take note of how the bold, bullets, indentations, large headlines and so on have remained intact. After reading this and Stephanie Chambers' CV, begin to work on your own two- and one-page CVs using a computer program like Word, following Gregory Miller's CV as your official template. It works, so don't change it!

Sample one-page CV

Gregory E. Miller
23 Hawthorn Gardens
London W11 2ZA
0171-623 45678
gem@aol.com

Summary of Qualifications
- Over ten years' experience in audio visual production management.
- Extensive experience in electronics training programs design and facilitation.
- Comprehensive knowledge of computers, software and networks.
- Extensive experience in new facility electronic systems design and implementation.

Work Experience
- **1993–Present**   **ABC Productions, London**
  Position: Manager Audio Visual Production
  Managed audio visual technology for a large, state-of-the-art conference centre. Recruited, trained and managed a staff of 12. Clients delighted.

- **1992–1993**   **ABC Production, London**
  Position: Instructor
  Responsible for the instruction of over 100 A-level Electronics students. Designed customized curriculums and selected appropriate textbooks.

- **1990–1992**   **Sound Systems, Glasgow**
  Position: Independent Contractor
  Designed all circuitry, circuit boards and installed the client's theatre system. During this time, also developed theatrical electrical systems for a cinema.

- **1986–1990**   **Newstime, London**
  Position: Electronic Systems Manager
  Designed, specified, installed and repaired all electronic systems, including telephone and satellite reception technology for this news network.

Education
- BA Electronics, University of Leeds

Awards and achievements
- Member, BECTU
- Member, Amalgamated Engineering and Electrical Union

References
- Available on request.

Sample one-page 'just-graduated' CV

Stephanie K. Chambers
Room 33
Student Halls
York University
York Y10 7BJ
01904 54321
stephaniek@aol.com

Summary of Qualifications
- Successfully completed a Business Administration and Marketing course.
- Over three years' work-study experience of administration and finance.
- Computer literate, with knowledge of Excel and Windows.
- Detailed and accurate organizational skills.

Education
- BS Business Administration and Marketing, York University, York

Work Experience
- **1995–Present**   **Modern Hotel, York**
  Position: Accounts Payable
  Responsible for processing all invoices and authorizing payments by cheque in accordance with the conference centre's activities. Reconcile daily statements and month-end balancing of payables. Maintain spreadsheets in Excel. Responsible for monthly accruals of £10,000.

- **1994–1995**   **Healthy Teeth Dental Practice, York**
  Position: Bookkeeper/receptionist
  Handled the preparation of invoices, payments by cheque, answered phone calls and greeted clients. Reconciled monthly bank statements. Maintained client files and kept information confidential. Prepared budgets for sums in excess of £40,000.

Awards and achievements
- Edited and contributed to Rag Week magazine
- Entertainments secretary for the Students' Union Committee

References
- Available on request.

Now that your two-page CV has been edited down to one page and is on white paper, what can give your CV the punch it needs to have to get its reader to act? Action words!

━━━━━━━ 9 ━━━━━━━

Use action words constantly throughout your CV. Take the time to be creative and use a thesaurus to avoid duplication

Make every word in your CV count. This is the same strategy that print advertisers use. Each word must say something important to the reader. After all, you, like an advertiser, want the reader to take action. An advertiser wants you to buy a product. You want a personnel, human resources or other manager to pick up the phone and call you.

Look back at the CVs on the previous pages. Underline the action words. Next, read the following list of action words that I have specially prepared to help get you started. Extract ten words from the list that will uniquely apply to you when you are preparing or revising your CV.

When you are creating a CV or covering letter, use action words. Summarize what actions you have taken at work and what the results were. Always provide numbers – figures for budgets or for projects, percentages, and increases. Numbers quantify your value or worth to a prospective employer. They show responsibility. For instance, saying you 'recruited, trained and managed the technical support staff' is a weak statement. A stronger statement is that you 'recruited, trained and managed 12 technical support staff.' To become more familiar with how to integrate numbers into your own CV, look back at the examples we have just been looking at and underline all the places where numbers were used.

Action words to use for effective CVs

accomplished	constructed	exceeded	integrated
achieved	consulted	executed	interpreted
acquired	contributed	expanded	interviewed
adapted	controlled	expedited	introduced
administered	coordinated	financed	invented
advanced	created	forecasted	invested
analysed	cut	formed	investigated
applied	decreased	formulated	led
arranged	delivered	found	liquidated
assessed	demonstrated	founded	located
assigned	designed	fulfilled	made
assisted	determined	generated	maintained
attained	developed	guided	managed
audited	devised	handled	marketed
bought	directed	headed	mediated
broadened	distributed	hired	minimized
brought	documented	identified	modified
calculated	doubled	implemented	monitored
centralized	earned	improved	motivated
collaborated	edited	improvized	negotiated
completed	eliminated	increased	obtained
composed	enforced	influenced	operated
conceived	engineered	initiated	ordered
concluded	established	instituted	organized
conducted	evaluated	instructed	originated
consolidated	examined	insured	overcame

oversaw	redesigned	set up	surveyed
participated	reduced	settled	taught
performed	regulated	shaped	terminated
pioneered	reinforced	showed	tested
planned	rejected	simplified	tightened
prepared	related	sold	traded
presented	renegotiated	solved	trained
prevented	reorganized	specified	transacted
processed	reported	sponsored	transferred
produced	represented	staffed	transformed
programmed	researched	standardized	translated
projected	reshaped	started	trimmed
promoted	resolved	stimulated	tripled
proved	restored	streamlined	undertook
provided	reviewed	strengthened	unified
published	revised	studied	used
purchased	revived	suggested	utilized
realized	saved	summarized	verified
recommended	scheduled	supervised	vitalized
reconciled	selected	supported	withdrew
recruited	served	surpassed	worked

Personal action words

Write ten sentences using ten action words that best describe your work history.

1 _____

2 _____

3 _____

4 _____

5 _____

6 _____

7 _____

8 _____

9 _____

10 _____

There is one final factor that determines a successful CV.

10

Target your CV to each particular company you write to and each position you apply for

The idea of targeting your CV should conjure up images of hitting the bull's-eye on a dartboard or shooting arrows at a practice target. It is exactly that kind of accuracy that is required every time you send out a CV. A common mistake is to produce one CV and send it out, unchanged, to all companies.

I'd like to give you an example of what I mean by targeting your CV. Consider a person applying for a management job at a manufacturing company. The CV will obviously need to communicate the job skills the person has acquired that demonstrate effective management of both employees and operations. Conversely, if this same person were to apply for a customer service management position, they must interject action words that demonstrate a successful track record servicing and maintaining customer satisfaction.

The first CV should not be sent to apply for the second position. It would not contain the customer service target language that would be likely to trigger the reader to offer an interview.

Now we'll do one together. Say someone is applying for the position of receptionist at a law firm. The position involves using the telephone and greeting clients. What skills should the person's CV emphasize? Mainly, the applicant should emphasize previous telephone experience and the ability, when under pressure, to interact with others and be pleasant.

If this same person also applied for a job as a receptionist to a company where they also wanted someone to do a little bookkeeping, what additional skills would be interjected into the CV sent for this vacancy? The applicant would need to demonstrate successful implementation of organizational and analytical skills. If at all possible, the CV should be slanted from a bookkeeping perspective.

In order to target your CV quickly on a daily basis, you need consistent access to a computer and laser printer. Keep copies of your CVs and covering letters on a disk so that you can transport the documents and edit them on a home, office or school computer. Store different versions of your CV so you have relevant ones ready for various applications. If you don't have easy access to a computer, contact a secretarial services company. They will help you edit your CV and covering letters for a minimum charge. Write each CV to target positions that you are applying for throughout your job search, and, where possible, choose to apply for jobs your previous work history qualifies you to do.

The electronic CV

Posting a CV on-line is a different thing altogether. Getting in on to the Internet can be achieved in various ways. Some online services, such as recruitment agencies, provide you with a screen form to fill out, which is added to their database. Other companies ask that you send them a copy of your original CV on disk or download it via a modem.

You will find that sites often offer you excellent and detailed help with writing your CV online and filling in application forms, but below are some general pointers to get you started.

Electronic CV-writing tips

* *Use nouns*

    Forget what I said in the previous section about action words and descriptives. The name of the game here is nouns. The people using these services ask their computers to search for key words, such as bio-tech, engineer, programmer, administrator.

• *Use key words*

    Think about the top ten key words that someone, if they were looking for you, would use to find you if they used the word search facility. Integrate all of those words into your CV. For instance, if you are a food and beverages manager, your key words may be:
    – restaurant
    – bar
    – food
    – service
    – hotel
    – banquets
    – dinning
    – menu
    – cuisine
    – food manager
    – beverage manager.

• *KISS*

    We came across this earlier, and it holds true for electronic CVs, too. Avoid decorative typefaces and too much underlining. In cyberspace, just give the facts!

- *Name and contact details first*

  You're selling yourself, so keep your contact information prominent in the CV so the reader knows where they can reach you when they like what they see.

- *Avoid jargon*

  Minimize the use of abbreviations and acronyms. Write using simple words that everyone knows and would commonly be used in your industry.

- *White spaces*

  The same is true of electronic as paper CVs – computer screens look good with lots of white spaces.

- *One-page CV*

  Keep it to one page if you have recently left school or graduated. One-, two- and three-page CVs are fine if you have been working a long time and have a great deal of experience.

- *Minimize e-mail*

  Do follow up an application, but avoid excessively e-mailing the companies you are applying to.

Covering Letters

For a covering letter to be effective, it has to be very calculated and follow key guidelines in much the same manner as a CV.

════════════ | | ════════════

An effective covering letter is divided into three distinct paragraphs

The three paragraphs each achieve a purpose:

1 *Attention*: the first paragraph gets the reader's attention with important facts or features about you;

2 *Benefit*: the second paragraph tells the company what the benefits would be of hiring you;

3 *Close for action*: the last paragraph must trigger the interview, so 'I shall look forward to meeting you to discuss my skills and the job in more detail. Meanwhile, if you should have any questions, please call me on (give your phone number)'.

The first paragraph gets the reader's attention. This is where you mention a few outstanding, relevant facts or features about yourself. I remember a young man applying this advice after one of my seminars in America a few years ago. He had cleaned pools in South Florida all the time he was at college there, but he felt there was nothing about cleaning pools that would get anyone's attention in his covering letter for a job application. I asked how many pools he serviced when he first started. '35,' he replied. Then he remembered how, over the years, he acquired more customers because many of the pool owners referred him to their friends. Eventually, he had over 50 customers. Now, all of a sudden, he realized that he did have something significant to say about his achievements as a pool cleaner. No longer was he an inexperienced recent college graduate. He began to realize the special skills it took to maintain customers, acquire new ones and be a loyal employee for many years. He put these down in his covering letter, and was offered a position at a major telecommunications company, making $16,000 the first year there! Noting these skills was a world away from thinking of himself as being *just* a pool cleaner and seeing that as a limitation. The example of his covering letter shows how he followed my guidelines, portraying himself as the success story he, in fact, was.

The second paragraph of a covering letter tells the personnel, human resources or other manager what the benefits of hiring you would be. This is where you don't just give them facts, you must give them corresponding benefits as well. For example, it is not enough to say you have received extensive training (that is a fact). Give them a benefit, too. In so many words, let them know that because you are trained, they will save valuable time and be able to give top priority to other department projects. If you can communicate this, you're very close to getting the job!

Never state a fact, feature or advantage without stating a benefit of this to the reader. Without a corresponding benefit, the person you're writing to may not realize how it will profit them. This can be stated more strongly: facts, features and advantages mean nothing without benefits. If you master the technique of fact + benefit = results, you will have an explosive tool for interviews. Hopefully, the only problem you'll have is deciding which job offer to accept.

Because this technique is extremely valuable, be absolutely sure you are clear on how to construct, write and state a fact plus a corresponding benefit. Practise this by filling in the Fact-to-benefit worksheet on page 46. The first couple are done for you as examples of how to do this.

Sample covering letter

Joe Adams
37 South Drive
Hollywood Beach, FL 33020
Hampshire GU32 7RA

12 January, 1995

Ms Jane Melville
ABC Company
100 Company Boulevard
Miami, FL 33138

Dear Ms Melville

Re: Sales Associate Position

My CV, which I have enclosed, presents my training and experience in sales and customer service over the past two years. I have successfully managed 35 customer accounts and increased my customer base over a period of time to more than 50 with Blue Water Pool Cleaning Service, where I currently work. This experience has given me a solid background in sales and customer service that will enable me to benefit your company.

The particular skills I have needed and developed in my work are creativity, adaptability and initiative. I have shown myself to be a self-starter as it is important to be resourceful and establish immediate rapport and long-lasting relationships with clients and colleagues to get the job done and grow the business. I can thus fit into a team quickly and effectively with little need for further training.

I hope, having read the above and considered my CV, that you will consider me for the Sales Associate position. I look forward to meeting you to discuss my skills and the job in more detail. Meanwhile, if you should have any questions, please call me on (954) 555 4493.

Yours sincerely,

Joe Adams
Enc.: CV

Fact-to-benefit worksheet	
Fact, feature or advantage	*Corresponding benefit*
1 I'm just out of college.	1 You will have an eager, energetic employee who will grow with, and be dedicated to, the company.
2 I have ten years' experience.	2 There will be minimum time wasted in training. I will begin to be productive virtually immediately.
3 I studied that at college.	
4 Computers are my speciality.	
5 My previous boss liked how organized and professional I was.	
6 I haven't missed a day of work in two years.	
7 I always worked overtime whenever my boss asked.	
8 In my spare time, I do volunteer work for the Red Cross, giving workshops on AIDS awareness to teenagers.	
9 My parents taught me responsibility at an early age.	
10 My hobbies include sports and computers.	

In my opinion, the third paragraph of a covering letter is the shortest and easiest to construct, but many people seem to have a hard time doing it. Close for action, just like all the advertising mail you get for all those incredible once-in-a-lifetime offers. Prompt the reader to take action by mentioning that you look forward to meeting them and then give your phone number so it is really easy for them to take the next step.

Do not rely on weak phrases such as 'Hope to hear from you soon' or phrases that set you up for failure, such as, 'Thank you for your consideration. I'll call you next week.' If they know you are going to call, they are going to make sure you don't get through. It is always better to get them to call you. When they do call you, it is an indication that there is something about you they want. This places you in a much better position to negotiate and sell yourself at the interview. If you must call them, don't announce that you will do so in your letter. Just plan on calling them about eight to ten business days after posting your letter. If you faxed it to them, call within six to eight days if you have not heard from the company.

Now that you have read this chapter, please do not try to get a job with your CV and covering letter alone!

═══ 12 ═══

The purpose of the CV and covering letter is to get you the interview

Even the best CV and covering letter in the world are not likely to result in the job being offered to you there and then. Most companies do not employ people sight unseen. A CV and covering letter, then, are just selling tools to get you an interview. The interview is where you sell yourself and secure the job offer.

Let's review what we have learned in this chapter:

- How to design a one-page CV.
- How to produce a professional-looking CV on white paper.
- The importance of using action words.
- How to target your CV.
- How to create a covering letter, dividing it into three distinct paragraphs:
  1 get their attention;
  2 state the benefits to the company of the facts about you;
  3 close for action, prompting the reader to call you for an interview and giving them your phone number.
- don't try to get a job with a CV and covering letter alone – their only purpose is to get you an interview.

4
Developing leads and networking

Generating new leads and contacts is the single most crucial activity you must perform daily to get the job you want. Spend your waking hours developing leads, contacts and networking. Getting the job you want is mostly a numbers game.

Gambling casinos work on the same system. Last year, I visited Monte Carlo and, for the first time ever, spent an evening at a casino. Knowing I was inexperienced, I immediately determined that feeding coins into a slot machine was my best bet. After cashing £30 for French ten-franc pieces, I cautiously began to drop one coin in at a time. I learned quickly. Every time I hit with one coin, I only received a measly two or three coins back. After taking notice of the odds and combination chart posted on the machine, I realized that, in order to win a larger payback, I had to risk more coins. Winning two and three coins was not good enough for me! I was determined to win big and so began placing two- and three-coin bets. After ten or more bets, nothing. I was concerned. Then it happened –a three-coin hit! The payback was at least 50 coins or better. I was hooked! Discovering my numbers game worked, I continued to play until 3.00 in the morning, winning a total of over £300!

Tom Jackson, author of *Guerrilla Tactics in the Job Market*, agrees that job hunting is mostly a numbers game. He says, 'Every job campaign looks much like this: NO, NO, NO, NO, NO, NO, NO, NO, NO, NO, NO, NO, YES!'

Just like in a casino, every time you are searching for a new job, the process will be a long series of losses followed by a win. At least in the job market you have better odds – you only have to get one yes! So please don't take the casino illustration out of context. I'll admit, I was lucky that night. However, the fact remains, if you don't play the numbers game, you can't win!

I am aware that many people have a deep-rooted fear of rejection. Although these people would agree that, in principle, getting a job is mostly a numbers game, they will never achieve their goals because when they are turned down this is taken as a personal rejection. When such moments are viewed negatively, the job search process actually goes into reverse. Someone thinking this way will apply for fewer jobs in order to be shielded from further disappointments. This is counterproductive to achieving the desired goal.

When you are turned down for a job, this is actually a positive experience, in much the same way my early failure in the casino helped me to become a winner. Every loss I had put me one bet closer to a 50-coin win. For every no you get, you are one step closer to that one yes! Just like losses have to be accepted when you put your money into a slot machine, receiving noes when you are applying for jobs comes with the territory.

Brian Tracy, in his tape series *The Science of Self-confidence*, states that 'If you are not failing, you're not trying.' Don't be afraid to fail. Reassess your attitude towards failure. Unfortunately, as children, we often learn the wrong message about failure. We are punished for failure in many ways and quickly learn that failure is to be avoided. As adults, we should have discovered the opposite – that success is always preceded by failure.

Thomas Edison, in his quest to make a lightbulb, performed thousands of experiments. Somewhere near experiment 10,000, he created the first lightbulb. Someone asked him how he felt about his failures. He responded, 'I learned 10,000 ways how not to make a lightbulb.' Through his thousands of experiments, Edison discovered that success is a numbers game. Try something long enough, in a number of different ways, making intelligent guesses along the way, and you will eventually succeed. History is marked with great failures who became great successes. The books are full of people who have failed often enough to learn how to succeed.

You can tell how high or low a person is going to go in life by how they respond to rejection and failure. Losers see failure as indicative of their lack of talent and abilities. They become disappointed easily. Eventually, they become preoccupied with taking no further risks in life. They shield themselves from further disappointments. Brian Tracy states, 'People that fear failure put their lives into reverse. They try fewer and fewer things and success avoids them.' Winners, on the other hand, welcome failure. They realize that triumph over failure brings them over the edge to success.

How do you view a glass of drink? Is it half empty or half full? Do you view a failed application as one step closer to defeat or one step closer to winning? Make a commitment today to increase the number of noes you are going to get. You are now on the fast track to getting the job you want.

Although you may agree with what I am saying in principle, you may still not have resolved a common but important question: 'How do I remain motivated, even in a slump?'

In order to keep yourself from becoming depressed or to cheer yourself up, should you find you have slipped into this state unawares, you must reward yourself when you meet daily goals. Realize that today's objective, in essence, is not to get a job. Instead, today's objective is to perform the correct, consistent job-seeking activities you are learning in this book. Meeting your daily goals is your only concern, as getting the job you want will be the automatic result of having done this.

Becoming depressed is a result of focusing on a job offer. Your mind can play tricks on you. It says you will only be happy when you get a job offer. The truth really is that your mind needs reprogramming. True happiness and well-being are achieved by accomplishing each day's objectives. Someone who meets their daily goals has the confidence that a job offer will result. This is the law of cause and effect in action: what you get back is a direct result of what you put in; or, meet your daily job-seeking goals and you will get a job.

13

Secure 6 new leads a day (30 a week) and send them a covering letter and your CV (read on for where to find new leads)

This formula for success involves selecting 30 new leads a week that are compatible with your particular career goals. That is only six new leads per day, working five days a week. The total comes to 120 leads for a month. Accelerate your fast track to success even more by generating six new leads a day, working seven days a week. The total then is 180 leads for the month! It can be done, and your success is virtually guaranteed.

14

Secure ten leads a week from the newspapers' recruitment sections, sending a covering letter and your CV

Newspapers' recruitment sections must comprise only one third of your total new leads. Around 85 per cent of all jobs available are never published. Therefore, if you rely on the newspaper for all of your leads, you're missing out on 85 per cent of the jobs actually available. Worse yet, if 100 per cent of the people looking for work are reading the newspaper and vying for the 15 per cent of jobs available by this means, where does that leave you?

15

Secure ten leads a week from making cold calls

'Cold calling' is a method that, when used well, will get you creatively networking and connect you with the other 85 per cent of the jobs that are unpublished. The term comes from what some salespeople do, marketing certain types of products door to door, and often has bad associations with imitating pushiness, but my version of cold calling is different. I use this term to mean simply dropping in on ten businesses you would like to work for and leaving your CV with a secretary, supervisor or manager.

While you are there, you can ask for the name or business card of the person who is responsible for recruiting people for the jobs you are interested in. Then, when you return home, post each contact your covering letter and another CV. Better yet, try to see these people while you are there. The law of averages dictates that you will get an on-the-spot interview for every few cold calls you make. These interviews could have taken weeks to arrange if you had relied on more traditional methods, making you weeks ahead of your competition.

After hearing this, I know already what you are thinking. 'He must be mad! There's no way I'm going to walk into a strange office and hand out my CV! I'll just stick to the newspapers and answer adverts from home.' This is quite a natural response, but, remember, 85 per cent of all jobs available are never published. If that does not convince you, let me tell you a true story of an unemployed man who found a creative way to tap into the unpublished job market. Early one Monday morning, this man left his home to go to the airport. One small thing though – he did not have a plane to catch. Instead, on arriving at the terminal in his sharpest business suit, he began to hand out copies of his CV to the executives queuing to check in for their flights. One executive who was there that day admired his tenacity and creative spirit so much that he called the man back a few days later and offered him a job. So, it pays to be proactive and get creative!

Remember, if all the job-seekers are applying for jobs by replying to ads in the newspapers, and these are for only 15 per cent of the available jobs, the competition for those jobs is staggering.

The top five reasons for cold calling

There are many personal benefits to cold calling, but here are the top five.

1 You tap into a huge market of available jobs 'unpublished'.

2 You reduce the competition you are up against because the other 90 per cent of people are at home reading the newspaper ads, competing for 15 per cent of the jobs.

3 You remain current and learn of new jobs as they happen.

4 You establish a network and can gain valuable contacts who often turn into lifelong business connections that will help you in the future.

5 It helps you maintain a positive self-image as you get out daily, dressed smartly, and remain part of the business community. (Sitting at home in your bathrobe day in and day out can have a devastating effect on your feelings of self-worth.)

Here's how to cold call. The night before you go, plan your strategy. For instance, 'Tomorrow, I will park my car just off the High Street and visit every company within a radius of a five-minute walk' or 'Tomorrow, I will visit all the companies on the new office park on the outskirts of town' or 'Tomorrow I will drive to the north of the town centre and visit the following companies located in that area.'

The next day, get up early, dress smartly and prepare mentally as if you were going for an actual interview. Arrive at your first planned location as early as 8.45 or 9.00. Bring with you 15 to 20 CVs, neatly placed in a professional-looking black folder. When you arrive at the reception area of each company, things should go something like this.

First, introduce yourself: 'Good morning, my name is _____.' Next, state your purpose: 'I don't have an appointment. However, I would like to speak with the person in charge of hiring supervisors in the customer service department. Who would that be, please?'

At this point, be prepared! They may contact the person in charge who will grant you an interview on the spot, but the opposite may happen, too. They may say, 'I'm sorry, that manager will not see anyone without an appointment.' When this happens you have two choices. You can politely persist, as they just might sympathize with you and call the manager in to meet you. Alternatively, you could simply ask for the name or business card of that person and leave your CV with the receptionist. Then, when you go home, send the person a covering letter and another CV. Then you achieve double name recognition!

Be aware that some companies can be very difficult to infiltrate. In these cases, it would be in your best interest to call the managers concerned and simply request to see them for 20 minutes to find out more about the company. This tactic very often works. Let them know you are on a mission to learn more about their influential company and not necessarily looking for a job there at the moment. This method helps you to get in the front door, get your name known, make a friendly contact and sell yourself in a subtle but effective way.

There is another way to tactfully muscle your way into 'heavily fortressed' companies, but whether or not it is for you depends on how much time you are willing to spend on doing this. This option is to offer to be a volunteer. Telephone, write or just show up at the company. Explain that you have certain skills you are seeking to develop and/or, perhaps, write a paper about. Further, explain that you would be willing to volunteer a certain number of hours each week in related activities. They won't have to pay you, so how could they refuse?

I know of a number of people who have succeeded with this tactic. Some were eventually asked to stay with the company and were offered full-time positions. It seems like everyone wants to be paid before they'll do something, but success does not always come in easy and obvious ways. Hector, for instance, volunteered in this way at the head office of a major international airline. As you may or may not know, getting a job at the head office of an airline without first paying your dues at the airport working on a customer service desk or as a flight attendant is practically impossible. Initially, he worked two days a week in the human resources department. He looked and acted as professionally – in some cases more so – as the other employees in the department. He arrived at 9.00 am sharp. His clothes were clean, pressed and sophisticated, and his grooming impeccable. Best of all, Hector's work was executed in a timely, organized and well-thought-out fashion. Cutting a long story short, after only a couple of months of working on a volunteer basis, a nearby department announced a last-minute need for a new supervisor. Guess who got the job? Correct: Hector!

Keep in mind, as I'm sure you already have, that not everyone is going to get a job offer after volunteering. However, also recognize nevertheless that, as a result, you will have developed new skills and will be more marketable to another organization. The company you volunteered for will also serve as an excellent reference. Often, medical research charities, government agencies and other non-profit-making organizations are eager to find   people willing to volunteer. When your work performance is of exceptional quality in this type of situation, your career has nowhere to go but up.

Finally, on leaving the office you have cold called, thank the receptionist for their time and write their name down as well. Treat receptionists kindly and they will become your allies. When you telephone the company, remind the receptionist who you are and they will make sure your call is put through to the right person rather than trying to fob you off.

To help you prepare, here is a cold calling script for you in its entirety. Practise it, role playing with a friend the night before you intend going on some visits. There will then be minimal stage fright the next day. By the way, the more cold calls you make, the easier it becomes.

Cold calling script assuming full cooperation

Job-seeker *(to the receptionist)*: Good morning/afternoon, my name is _____. I don't have an appointment. However, I would like to speak with the manager in charge of the _____ department. Who would that be, please?

Receptionist: That is Ms/Mr _____. What is this regarding?

Job-seeker: Please let Ms/Mr _____ know I called by to ask a few questions to gain more insights into a career in his/her department. I wanted to ask his/her advice about getting into/developing my skills further in this area.

Receptionist: Please wait one moment. I'll call and see if she/he is in. *(He/she dials.)* Please be seated. Ms/Mr _____ will be down in a moment to see you.

Job-seeker: Thank you for your help. Your name is? Thank you very much, _____.

(Manager comes to lobby. Job-seeker initially mentions why they have come, as explained to the receptionist, above. Job-seeker begins to enquire about the department, advice on where his/her skills would fit in, potential positions available and if the manager would be able to refer them to other departments and/or companies. A preliminary interview begins. Job-seeker closes, arranging another appointment to pursue employment further and asks the manager for a business card or their extension number so they can contact them directly.)

Cold calling script: coping with a challenge

Job-seeker *(to the receptionist)*: Good morning/afternoon, my name is _____ . I don't have an appointment. However, I would like to speak with the manager in charge of the _____ department. Who would that be, please?

Receptionist: That is Ms/Mr _____. What is this regarding?

Job-seeker: Please let Ms/Mr _____ know I called by to ask a few questions to gain more insight into a career in his/her department. I wanted to ask his/her advice about getting into/developing my skills further in this area.

Receptionist: Please wait one moment. I'll call and see if she/he is in. *(He/she dials)* I'm sorry, Ms/Mr _____ cannot see you right now.

Job-seeker: I understand completely. Please pass my CV on to him/her to look at. By the way, do you have a business card for Ms/Mr _____ or one for the company?

(Receptionist hands job-seeker a business card.)

Thank you for your help. Your name is? Thank you very much, _____ .

(Job-seeker leaves and writes down the receptionist's name and other pertinent notes in a notebook before going on to their next call.)

The same process of cold calling, as just described, can be adapted to marketing yourself by telephone. (I call it 'tele-self-marketing'.)

16

Secure five leads per week from the Yellow Pages, the phone book or a business directory.

Call the businesses you would like to work for and send them a covering letter and your CV. Using tele-self-marketing in this way means that, once again, you tap into the huge market of unpublished jobs available. Just by making telephone calls, you are gathering important information and making contacts.

After you have selected a category in the *Yellow Pages*, begin calling the businesses given in that category. Introduce yourself in the same way that was suggested above for cold calling in person, stating your purpose. Ask to speak with the person in charge of hiring people for the job you want. Try to get through to them and arrange a meeting, or find out their name and send them a copy of your covering letter and CV.

To help you prepare yourself, here is a tele-self-marketing script for you in its entirety. As you did for cold calling, practise with a friend the night before. With practise, you will minimize any stage fright. Remember, the more phone calls you make, the easier it becomes.

Tele-self-marketing script assuming full cooperation

Job-seeker *(to the switchboard operator)*: Good morning/ afternoon, my name is _____. I am calling because I would like to speak with the manager in charge of the _____ department. Who would that be, please?

Switchboard operator: That is Ms/Mr _____. Please hold while I transfer you.

(Job-seeker is transferred to the manager's secretary.)
Secretary: Good morning/afternoon. Ms/Mr _____'s office.

Job-seeker*(sounding confident)*: Good morning/afternoon, I am _____. Ms/Mr _____, please.

Secretary: What is this with regard to?

Job-seeker: Please let Ms/Mr _____ know I'm calling to ask a few questions to gain more insight into a career in his/her department. I wanted to ask his/her advice about getting into/developing my skills further in this area.

Secretary: Please hold the line one moment. Ms/Mr _____ will be with you shortly. *(The secretary puts you on hold.)*

Job-seeker: Thank you very much.

(Manager takes the phone call. Job-seeker initially repeats what he/she told the secretary. Job-seeker begins to enquire about the department, advice on where his/her skills would fit in, potential positions available and if the manager would be able to refer them to other departments and/or companies. Job-seeker closes, arranging to meet to talk about this in person and offering to take the manager to lunch.)

Tele-self-marketing script:coping with a challenge

Job-seeker *(to the switchboard operator)*: Good morning/afternoon, my name is _____ . I am calling because I would like to speak to the manager in charge of the _____ department. Who would that be, please?

Switchboard operator: That is Ms/Mr _____ . Please hold while I transfer you.

(Job-seeker is transferred to the manager's secretary.)

Secretary: Good morning/afternoon. Ms/Mr _____'s office.

Job-seeker *(sounding confident)*: Good morning/afternoon, I am _____ . Ms/Mr _____ , please.

Secretary: What is this with regard to?

Job-seeker: Please let Ms/Mr _____ know I'm calling to ask a few questions to gain more insight into a career in his/her department. I wanted to ask his/her advice about getting into/developing my skills further in this area.

Secretary: Please hold the line one moment. *(The secretary puts you on hold.)* I'm sorry, Ms/Mr _____ is not available at the moment.

Job-seeker: I really would like to speak to him/her now if it's possible. I can hold a moment more.

Secretary: I'm sorry. He/she is very busy right now.

Job-seeker: I understand. When would be a good time to call again? Later this morning, or this afternoon?

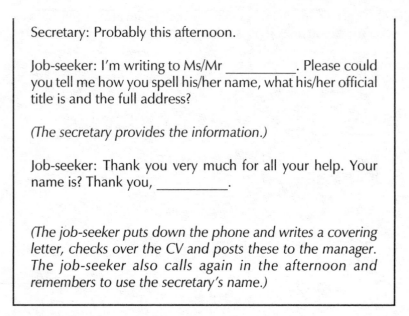

Secretary: Probably this afternoon.

Job-seeker: I'm writing to Ms/Mr _____ . Please could you tell me how you spell his/her name, what his/her official title is and the full address?

(The secretary provides the information.)

Job-seeker: Thank you very much for all your help. Your name is? Thank you, _____ .

(The job-seeker puts down the phone and writes a covering letter, checks over the CV and posts these to the manager. The job-seeker also calls again in the afternoon and remembers to use the secretary's name.)

Highly efficient secretaries are probably the biggest obstacle when cold calling or tele-self-marketing. Remember, though, that they are only doing their job. Be polite and do not take it personally. However, there are ways to encourage cooperation from a secretary. One way is to sound authoritative. If you sound important and professional (not weak or scared), in many instances you will be put right through to the manager, no questions asked. Also, you can call before or after business hours. At these times the secretary will not be there and the manager will usually answer the phone themself. I have had tremendous cooperation from switchboard operators. Call the operator and ask authoritatively, 'What's the extension number for Ms/Mr_____'s office?' or 'What is the number for Ms/Mr_____'s direct line?' Sound like you work in the building and you have lost their number. It works. Then you can either call the number again and simply ask for the extension number you were given, or use the direct line number.

What do you do if the switchboard operator or secretary asks you to leave your name and number? Don't! If you leave your name and number, they've got you. They know, then, not to put you through when you call back. Do this politely, otherwise you could hinder your chances when you call again and of getting the secretary's cooperation. To avoid leaving my name and number, I usually say, 'Oh, no, it's OK. I'll try again later. What would be the best time to call back?'

There is a way to double your leads when cold calling and tele-self-marketing. Here's how to do it. After you have spoken with somebody at a company and have established rapport, ask them for a referral: 'What other companies or who else would you recommend I contact?' Most are pleased to help a job-seeker and will duly give you names of people and companies. Sometimes they are even located in the same office building.

A referral has a magic all its own. You then have a special key to getting into a company. In most cases, the receptionist will put you through to the person you need to speak to or ask them if they'll see you more speedily, asking fewer questions, and the manager will also be less reticent to see or speak to you.

I term a referral a 'warm call'. It is superior to a cold call. Generally speaking, they have a higher potential for success than do cold calls. You can, of course, also ask for referrals from friends, acquaintances, relatives and friends of friends.

As you can see, with the methods we have been discussing, when you are unemployed, you should not be wasting important business hours sitting at home waiting for companies to respond to applications you've made in response to newspaper adverts. Further, you can make valuable use of your evening and weekend hours by networking and attending community functions.

17

Secure five leads by networking – attend all relevant business association meetings and community organizations' functions

Networking is the important process of getting out and about, attending a variety of community events. Call your local Chamber of Commerce. They may permit you to attend a meeting or two at no charge. The Chamber will also be able to give you the names and phone numbers of local branches of professional associations. You can call each of them and ask if you could attend their next meeting.

Keep in mind that there are many professional associations that relate to your career (directly or indirectly) and they usually meet monthly. You may or may not know about them. Do some research. The local branches of such groups will welcome a new face.

Networking resources

Here is an expanded list of creative resources for networking and obtaining referrals.

- Professional associations
- Friends
- Relatives
- Neighbours
- The Internet
- Colleagues, freelance, agency and contract staff
- Priest, rabbi, minister and church organizations
- Teachers
- Conference centres and professional fairs, such as the Motor Show in London
- Job clubs
- Clubs
- Professionals: doctors, lawyers, bankers and so on
- Previous employers' competitors
- Employment agencies
- Exchange e-mail with professional members of an online service

There is a proliferation of employment agencies, with branches in all major cities and towns. Agencies are profit-making businesses and make their money by charging substantial fees to the employer for finding and placing appropriate people. However, always check before signing anything as there are some agencies that work in reverse, charging you if they find you a job and you are accepted for it. Read everything thoroughly – and be sure this is what you want to do.

In most instances, an agency takes over the responsibilities of marketing yourself for you. This may sound like the easy way out – it saves you time, frustration and rejection, and you still get a job. However, be aware that there can be drawbacks. Realize that you could be encouraged to take a job that you normally would not have wanted, as agents develop a keen ability to sell jobs to people. You could end up in a job that will set your career back instead of forward.

I recommend using agencies as only a small part of your total plan. If managed carefully, they can work effectively for you. With your own efforts and theirs, you will have more leverage when negotiating to take or not to take a job offer that they recommend.

Job hunting on the Internet

An electronic-based job search is an important addition to a conventional job search, but should not replace it. That said, there are many sites on the Internet that will help you find a job. Individual sites can be focused on one area or list vacancies from all over the world.

'But how do I get a job using the Internet?' you may ask. First, it is assumed that you have access to a computer, a modem and a service provider. If you don't, see if you can use the facilities of a school, office, friend or a job club. In other words, there is little excuse not to expand your job search to the Internet.

Once you have logged on, you may locate information by using search engines such as *Alta Vista* and *Yahoo*. You do this by entering such general key words as 'recruitment' or 'employment' or more specific ones – 'genetics', say – at the search prompt. Listings of recruitment agencies and so on are in no particular order, so you simply scroll through the selection and click on entries that interest you to find out more.

Try Guardian RecruitNet through the search engine or at *http://recruitnet.guardian.co.uk* for a listing of job opportunities organized into categories. You can also use the Early Bird facility, which e-mails you with details of any vacancies that match up with your description of the kind of job you are looking for. Another example is Reed Personnel Services, at *http://www.reed.co.uk*, which has facilities that enable you to register with them online and to e-mail and send them application forms online, too. Employers can also register vacancies, of course, and your details will be passed to them if your experience etc fits with their needs. These are just two examples of the kinds of sources of information that are available on the Internet, so I am sure you will see how useful this hi-tech form of job hunting could be to you. If you haven't tried it, go ahead – people are finding jobs using this means every day.

Besides the Internet, a job-seeker has various other hi-tech options for communicating with prospective employers. When used effectively, they can speed up your job search and get you a job in even less than 30 days!

Tim used this book when he was searching for a job. He got a job in only 14 days, using current technology to his advantage. His goal was to work in pharmaceutical sales for one of the top 15 drug companies. Using a pharmaceutical directory, he began calling each one of the top drug companies. As he called, he used the tele-self-marketing script given earlier in this chapter. Along with the standard information, he also got the manager's fax number. When he put the phone down after speaking to him, he immediately faxed his CV and a covering letter using his computer. He followed this up at the end of the day by posting printed out copies of what he had faxed. Within the first four hours of faxing covering letters and CVs, he received three phone calls asking him to come for an interview. One company saw him within a few days of having received his faxes and letters. He was offered a job within two weeks of the very first day of his job search.

Hi-tech communication protocol

- Fax your CV and covering letter. Follow these up with normal printouts of what you faxed, sending them the same day.
- When faxing, avoid gimmicky attention-getter cover pages.
- Don't overdo your faxing. One fax of your CV to any one person is enough.
- Send your CV as an e-mail attachment. However, only do so if this has been requested by the manager.
- Do not send a photo of yourself as an e-mail attachment.
- Use e-mail for networking purposes. Drop short messages to those with e-mail addresses, enquiring about potential positions, referrals and advice.
- Only send one or two e-mails to the same person, then wait until the person chooses to correspond with you.
- Keep your e-mails professional – do not let the content become too personal.
- Scannable CVs. Most employers receive hundreds of CVs weekly and monthly. Many keep track of them in electronic databases that scan and store your CV. For the scanner to work, remember:
  - to avoid graphics;
  - to avoid shading and shadowing;
  - that stapled and folded CVs do not scan well;
  - that bold scans well;
  - that typefaces in point sizes 10–14 are best;
  - to print on one side only;
  - to use key nouns that are important to your industry and career;
  - to use the jargon of your field;
  - to keep it simple.

Having described the activities we have discussed in this chapter, you now know that getting a job is not a passive process that depends on luck; it can be a full-time job.

════ 18 ════

Develop sources of leads relentlessly, including use of the Internet (do this daily from 9.00 until 5.00 or, if you are working, in evenings and at weekends), until you achieve your goal

When you are serious about finding a good job quickly, do not waste precious time doing unrelated tasks during business hours. Have you ever noticed how, when you are looking for a job, even cleaning the house becomes tempting? Really, be honest about this! Don't be a procrastinator. Take charge of your life! In the words of Dr Denis Waitley, author of *The Psychology of Winning*, 'Winners make it happen! Losers let it happen!'

Let's review what we have learned in this fourth chapter.

- Secure 30 or more leads per week.
- Use the newspaper to find ten leads.
- Cold call ten leads per week.
- Secure five leads per week from the *Yellow Pages* or a professional directory.
- Gain five leads per week using networking resources.
- Work relentlessly at generating new leads, using the Internet if you can. Do not perform unrelated activities during business hours.

5
How to sell yourself at the interview

The interview – no matter how you describe it – is purely a selling situation, and you are the product. Remember, you are the greatest product you will ever sell!

The word 'selling', however, often has unwelcome connotations. It may conjure up thoughts of men in shiny suits selling used cars that don't work. Thus, the idea of selling yourself at an interview may not be something you would ever care to do. However, changing your attitude towards selling is essential if you are to become successful in interviews. This is because, as I said above, an interview is pure selling and so a knowledge of selling techniques is required if you are to do well. Life in general is selling, if you think about it. We are all selling something at some point: an idea to our children, someone we want a friend to go out with or one film rather than another when we go to the cinema. Here are five professional steps to selling that you should commit to memory. Implement them at an interview and you will have a clear winning advantage over the competition.

Five steps to self-selling

These five steps, altogether, happen every time you interview or encounter another person. They are as follows.

Step 1: Rapport

Get the interviewer to like you within the first 30 seconds. The way to do this is to use rapport-building techniques. These are tactics we all use to get others to like us. Here are four of these techniques.

Give a sincere compliment

You can comment on the friendly staff or even the artwork in the lobby. However, do not offer personal compliments. Avoid commenting on family photos on the desk or, if you are a gentleman, the jewellery a woman may be wearing. You could be guilty of treading in territory where you do not belong.

Ask an interest question

Interest questions are considered ice-breakers and should not be used to ask something personal. Rely on questions like, 'What did you think about that last goal in the game last night?' or 'When is the new addition to the building going to be completed?'

Make a brief statement

This is also considered to be an ice-breaker. A typical statement would be 'The rain this morning was the worst we've seen all year!' or 'Beautiful day today. Summer's nearly here'. I am sure you can think of hundreds more.

Names

As soon as possible, mention anyone you both may know or have in common. Name-dropping is always effective in building rapport. It creates a sense of friendship, of common ground. Name-dropping can be used at any time throughout the interview.

Step 2: Discovery

When you have an opportunity, ask discovery questions that elicit exact information about what qualities they are looking for in applicants. You'll need this information later. For example, ask the interviewer, 'What skills, in your opinion, are necessary to be successful at this position?'

Further, the purpose of the discovery stage is to find out what I call their DBM – 'dominant buying motive'. The DBM is the emotional reason for someone buying something. Research has proven that we all make decisions based on emotions and then rationalize our choices by finding some logic to them.

Before discussing how the DBM works in a self-selling interview situation, I would like to illustrate this point with a true story from a selling situation of another sort. A customer walks into a plumbing suppliers and finds a salesperson to help him pick out a hot water heater. Now, you may ask, 'What could possibly be emotional about buying a hot water heater?' The salesperson narrows the purchase options down to one of two units. The second unit costs considerably more, but it stores twice as much hot water as the first. The salesperson begins to ask good discovery questions and actually uncovers the emotional reason that, when satisfied, motivates the customer to buy. The questioning went something like this: 'How many people take showers in the morning at similar times?' The buyer said, 'Four'. 'Who is usually the last one to take a shower?' The buyer said it was him. At this point, the salesperson began to reminisce the emotions of taking cold showers. 'Don't you just hate it when you're the last one and the water is freezing? Especially on cold mornings! With the deluxe model you will never be in that situation again. It may cost a little more, but it is well worth it to have a warm shower.' Of course, the story ends with the buyer taking the deluxe model and the salesperson receiving a larger percentage in commission than he would have received for selling the other heater. Naturally, when the buyer gets back home, he, more than likely, will find some logical explanation for his purchase that he will tell the family. Usually emotions are not discussed. The logic could have been, 'It was reduced' or 'It was just the right dimensions to fit the place where the old one was'. The mistake often made is to give logical reasons when selling. Logic is not powerful enough to make someone act, but emotions are!

Transfer the lesson of this example to a self-selling interview situation. A job-seeker walks into the department manager's office for the final interview. The usual interview questions such as, 'Tell me about yourself', are asked. When the opportunity arises for the job-seeker to ask questions, the questions become tactful discovery questions, ones that gently probe to find out the manager's DBM. The exchange may go something like this: 'It seems that you and the assistant manager put in long hours here. What are the types of things that require so much overtime?' The manager responds honestly, 'We've been working overtime constantly for about six months. We just don't have enough help and the employees paid by the hour are limited in how many overtime hours they are allowed to do. We often have to finish up their reports just to stay on top of things.' The job-seeker has now found an emotion. The department manager is overworked, stressed and probably has very little leisure time. These are powerful, emotional situations that, if addressed, should result in a job offer. The key, however, is to address them without addressing them. The job-seeker responds, 'I can understand how demanding a department this large can be. I am not afraid of long hours or hard work. If I were to do some of this work, you would be able to focus on other departmental priorities.' It would be too obvious to come out and say, 'You will have more time off to be at home with your family.' However, the manager will draw that emotional conclusion from what you just said. In fact, one of my students once half-jokingly said, 'Give me a few weeks to settle in, and you may even find time for that weekend golf game you've been missing out on.' The manager laughed, and the job-seeker got the job!

Step 3: Problem

Along with your discovery questions, also learn about any special problem areas or needs that may impact this position. For example, ask the interviewer, 'What do you feel are the most difficult tasks associated with this position?' You already know about their general needs, as these are indicated by the position they are looking to fill, but ask probing, open-ended questions to find out about the sensitive areas. Such sensitive areas could include details such as that previous employees disliked being asked to work overtime or that, even though it is an accounting position, they are actually looking for someone with a good telephone manner as well as accounting abilities. If you don't dig out these special needs you will not know that they are important and that you should be selling yourself as a solution to them in the interview. Don't rely on the interviewer to automatically tell you everything they are looking for. An interviewer may purposely omit information, just to see if you demonstrate the qualities they are looking for without being prompted. Probing for these hidden problem areas, though, will, more than likely, get the interviewer to talk and create a positive impression of you in their minds.

Step 4: Solution

Now that you have gathered all the information necessary, begin to make statements that fit with and answer the prospective employer's exact needs. For example, explain to the interviewer, 'Earlier, you said that computer database and word processing experience would help a prospective manager in this department gain employee trust more rapidly. Over the past few years, I have been on several courses and so I will know or be able to learn about this department's programs very easily. I am sure that with these skills I will quickly be accepted.'

The steps described so far here may be best described as 'solution selling'. The solution step involves the job-seeker making things all right for the interviewer. The interviewer has a need (or a problem) and it is the task of the job-seeker to clearly communicate that they can fill that need and resolve the problem. The solution step is where you use all the information you've gathered in the previous steps to convince the interviewer that you can successfully meet the company's needs.

Step 5: Close for action

At the end of each interview – just like in the last paragraph of your covering letter – close with the aim of initiating some type of action. Never just say, 'Goodbye, thank you very much.' The most reasonable way to close is to ask what will happen next. Simply say to the interviewer, 'Based on what we have discussed here today, I'm positive that I can help you resolve the problems you are currently having. Could you tell me whether or not you

will be offering me a job here?' If the company has other requirements and interviews to be arranged, then you would close by
asking if you will be involved in the next step. If you don't ask,
don't expect to be told.

Interviewers want you to ask for the job. If you don't ask, how
will they know that you truly want to work there? Asking for the
job takes place towards the end of an interview. It's similar to a
salesperson who says, 'I'll go to the stock room and get you a
brand new one.' The salesperson assumes you are going to buy
the item.

That leads me on to the five different ways to ask for a job.
There is bound to be one or more that you will feel comfortable
with and use effectively. Here are five power closes.

Five power closes – asking for the job

1 The alternative close

Ask an 'either/or' question. For example, 'When would I start
work – before the Christmas holidays or after New Year?'

2 The misinformed close

Ask a question that requires the interviewer to correct you.
An example of this would be, 'Did you say Judy Walker is
who I would report to?' The interviewer would then respond,
'No, it is Susan Williams.' Of course you knew that, but it
caused the interviewer to see you as already working for the
company.

3 The minor point close

Ask a question secondary to asking for the job, such as 'How
many teams are there in the department? Would I be working
in one of the larger ones or with just one or two others?' Like
the last close, when they answer this question, you have them
visualizing you already working there.

---

4 The take for granted close

Make an assumption in your closing statement. For example you could say something like, 'I'll take a look at that programming problem at home and find that improvement you were interested in. I'll drop it off to you tomorrow.' By taking something for granted, as this example demonstrates, you are easing yourself into the desired result without the interviewer having to make a direct yes or no decision.

This way of closing an interview has as many variations as there are situations. When you are out buying something, you will notice how salespeople will often utilize the take for granted close to ease you into purchasing an item. To be truly effective in an interview, take things for granted from the minute you walk in the door. Look, act and speak as if you have been the one selected for the job.

5 The creating urgency close

Say things that make it urgent that they give you the job. For example, 'About how long will it take before you have evaluated all the candidates? I'd like to know because I have two other companies who appear to be interested in me. However, given a choice, your company is clearly the best match for my skills and career.'

If well rehearsed, this tactic will send a signal to the interviewer that you are in demand. As is the case with most things in life, the thing you have to compete for is the very thing you want. With the urgency close, you stimulate a need for haste and feelings of competition and demand.

Let's recap

OK, now a short quiz: what are the five steps to self-selling? They are:

1 rapport
2 discover
3 problem

4   solution

5   close for action.

You have just learned the five basic steps to self-selling. When we move on to role plays, I will ask you to role play these steps with a friend. To be effective, these five steps need to become second nature. Role playing them with a friend will help you accomplish this.

19

At an interview, there are two ways to learn about the company: by listening and by asking good questions

Good listening skills are a crucial factor in a successful interview. A person who listens well and asks good questions is perceived as being more intelligent than one who doesn't do these things. By putting good listening skills into action you are able to gather a wealth of information that will give you power. Picture a rocket blasting off from its launch pad. The rocket is you. The fuel is the information you gather.

We've all been in situations where we've failed to gather enough information and have been embarrassed by our ignorance. Possibly you can remember a time when you met someone you thought you might like to go out with. One time when you met, after only a brief discussion, you may have blurted out, 'I hate such and such band', or 'Museums are so boring'. You later find out that that band and museums are among that person's favourite things. Failure to gather information can result in failure to win friends and influence people. Listen for a while before you start talking about what skills you have and how they will help the company.

Good listening is demonstrated in a number of ways. Maintain good eye contact at all times. It is not necessary to stare the person down, but don't look at the floor, either. Take notes. This helps you to remember key bits of information that you will use later in the interview to sell yourself. It also delivers a message about you. You appear both reliable and professional. Using the correct body language will help you to listen. Nodding your head, leaning forward occasionally and other such gestures demonstrate you are concentrating on what the interviewer is saying.

The second way to gather information is to master the art of asking questions. Formulating good questions is not as easy as it sounds. Forget everything you learned as a child about asking questions. We all learned to ask 'closed questions', that is, questions that can be answered with just a 'yes' or a 'no'. Clearly, in adult communication, these questions gather little information. The rocket never gets off the ground because the fuel, the information, just isn't there.

Questions that do elicit information are called 'open questions'. Practise these with friends and family and you will see that it actually takes a little effort to frame questions in this way. Examples of open questions are, 'Why do you feel that way?', 'What would be the best way to handle that?' and 'Where do we go from here?' In general, open questions are formed with 'who', 'what', 'where', 'when', 'how' and 'why'. Using these kinds of questions gets you on your way to getting the information you need to influence the person you are speaking to.

Picture this: you have a friend you would like to go to the movies with on Saturday. You call the friend up and ask, 'Would you like to go to the movies?' You've set your friend up for a 'yes' or 'no' response. There are no other choices. Most people will respond with a 'no' to such a bald question. The odds of getting a 'yes' are considerably less. If you were to call the same person again, how would you express what you want to say using an open question? You could say, 'What are your plans for the weekend? Do you have time to go to the movies together, and what would you like to see?' The open question approach does not guarantee that you will get the desired response, it only increases your chances of getting a 'yes'. Sharpen your questioning skills using the open questions practice sheet.

Open questions practice sheet

Below, in the left-hand column, is a list of closed questions (questions that may be answered with a 'yes' or 'no'). In the right-hand column, reword the question to make it an open question (one that cannot be answered with a 'yes' or 'no'). Remember, open questions are usually formed using 'who', 'what', 'where', 'when', 'how' or 'why'.

Closed questions	Open questions
Example: Can I call you on Friday?	When can I call you on Friday?
1 Are there opportunities for promotion?	
2 Is there an induction course and other training for new employees?	
3 Do you need references?	
4 Will it take long to make your final decision?	
5 Is an annual report available?	
6 Is there a copy of the job description?	
7 Is there time for a tour of the building?	
8 Can I see the manager of the department before I leave?	
9 Can I take you out to lunch next week?	
10 Do you think it would be OK for me to call you back about that in a few days?	

The night before your interview, prepare your wardrobe and yourself. Prepare a list of questions you will ask at the interview. A person who asks good questions is perceived to be more intelligent than one who has no questions. It is quite all right to keep your questions in a black folder (the one you used for cold calling) and read from it, if you wish, at an interview. Following is a list of questions to get you started. Add to the list questions that obviously should be asked, in light of the company that has arranged the interview and the sort of job you are being interviewed for.

General questions to ask at the interview

1 What are the strengths of the company and the department?
2 What are the career opportunities for someone doing this job?
3 What kind of induction and other training is available to new employees?
4 What other departments will I interact with?
5 Who would I be reporting to?
6 What are the growth plans for this company and department?
7 What are the prospects for future promotions?
8 What opportunities are there to transfer from one division to another?
9 How long was my predecessor in this job? Why did they leave?
10 What kind of support staff is available?
11 How often will my performance be reviewed and when?
12 What is the policy regarding helping with course fees if I do an MBA or other course?
13 How would you describe the company culture? Mission? Vision? Values?
14 What is the company's management philosophy?
15 What expectations are there of the person in this position?
16 How often are staff expected to do overtime?

17 What percentage of the time will I be expected to devote to my various responsibilities?

18 What are the deadlines? Weekly? Monthly?

19 What opportunities – formal and informal – do employees have to offer feedback and share creative ideas?

20 When would I be starting?

Targeted questions to ask at the interview

Add questions of your own below. These questions should target precisely the company, position and situation that you are being interviewed for.

1 _____

2 _____

3 _____

4 _____

5 _____

6 _____

7 _____

8 _____

9 _____

10 _____

The night prior to your interview is the time to role play with a family member or friend. Going to an interview without some form of practice is like an actor going on stage without rehearsing the script. Practised simulation prepares you so you can be confident, composed and with a positive attitude at the interview.

20

Role play to rehearse for the interview

Ask a friend to pretend to be the interviewer. Ask your friend to pose the questions most frequently asked by interviewers. There follows a list of these questions. Next to the questions I have put two other columns so you can see the differences between a poor and an effective strategy for dealing with these common questions. After you have read my suggestions, you can create your own variation of the effective strategy to suite you and practise your responses by role playing an interview situation.

The questions most frequently asked by interviewers and strategies for answering them

Questions	Poor strategies	Effective strategies
1 Tell me about yourself.	Describe your childhood and the family pets, Rover and Fluffy.	Recall incidents as far back as you like, but they should demonstrate positive aspects of your upbringing, such as instilled values and a good work ethic. For example, 'When I was growing up, my parents both worked. We were taught very young to help out, take responsibility and work together.'
2 Why are you leaving your present job?	'Just between you and me, my boss and I haven't got on since day one!'	Never – and I mean never – speak from a negative standpoint, always a positive one. For example, 'The department I am in admittedly has no more advancement opportunities for years to come and I'm ready and eager to do more with my skills.'
3 Why do you want to work for us?	'I heard from a friend your company has staff reductions and other great benefits.'	'I did a bit of research on the company using the Internet before I applied. It was clear it stands for quality and is a leader in the industry. I know I would be really motivated to work hard for that kind of company.'
4 What do you do in your spare time?	'I watch TV.'	'I have many interests. I play squash and golf, I read a book or two a month, and I joined the amateur dramatics group a few months ago.'

Questions	Poor strategies	Effective strategies
5 What do you like about yourself?	'Er, I don't know.' (If *you* don't know, don't expect the interviewer to find something likeable about you.)	'I have a way of not letting things get me down. I don't take disagreements personally. I bounce back pretty fast, seeing the positive side of it.'
6 What is one negative you want to change in yourself?	'I hate to get up in the morning. I'm not a morning person.' (Guess what? You just lost the job!)	Find a negative that may also be construed as a positive. For example, 'My friends say I'm like a bull in a china shop sometimes. I take charge a lot and forget to get others involved. But, I'm working on it.'
7 Where do you want to be two or three years from now?	'Oh dear, I've never thought about things that far ahead. I'd just be happy with a job today.'	'I'd like to be in a growing company with a lot of learning opportunities. A company like yours where, when I work hard, I can prove myself ready to take on the next challenge and progress things.'
8 Why should I give you the job?	'Because it's why I went to college. I know all about this.' (So have the other ten candidates.)	Find something that is uniquely you, something another candidate would have a difficult time competing with. For example 'You should hire me because I like to take pride in my work. It's something ingrained in me by my parents. For this reason you are assured quality work.'

The answers in the 'Poor Strategies' column may have seemed a bit over the top, but they are replicas of similar incidents from actual interviews. Someone who gives these sorts of answers should not be considered ignorant. It is apparent that they have simply not practised and so are not prepared. Inappropriate comments such as these are often the result when someone is thinking off the cuff. Let's face it, the best of us have all said things we should not have when we have been afforded no time to prepare. It is for this exact reason that our system is built around dress rehearsals, practice and role plays. Practise! Practise! Practise!

Now you are ready to set up a role play. Before your friend arrives, make the following preparations:

- list the questions you will ask the interviewer;
- list the questions you anticipate the interviewer will ask you;
- list your answers to the questions the interviewer will ask you;
- review the Five steps to self-selling (see page 69).

When your friend arrives, give them a general description of the role they will be playing and the company they will be representing. Also, hand them a list of the sorts of questions you anticipate will be asked of you so they can drill you.

Begin the role play by having your interviewer greet you and bring you to their office. Your objective in the role play is to take the interviewer through the Five steps to self-selling. Your other objective is to have clear, concise answers to the questions the interviewer will ask of you. Relax! Have fun and make mistakes. You'll have two left feet initially, but who cares? It's better to feel that way now than at the interview. Role play for about two hours five or six times.

21

Arrive for the interview 15 minutes early, do not arrive late or on time

A good candidate arrives at an interview at least 15 minutes early. When you arrive on time, you are actually arriving late! When you arrive early, you have arrived in plenty of time to fill out any important pre-interview forms. You also have time to watch and learn, observing the company.

22

While filling out pre-interview forms, sit in a relaxed but slightly formal way and, rather than read magazines in the waiting area, read the notes you have been using to prepare yourself for the interview

Besides giving you time to fill out pre-interview forms, there are many other benefits to arriving early. First, you are not frantic if the traffic is bad and there is a lack of parking space; you arrive relaxed. You are therefore in a better frame of mind to focus on making the interview go really well. Second, you provide yourself with time to observe the company, gather valuable information and rehearse in your mind your exact interview performance, rather like actors rehearse lines in their mind while they wait to go on stage. An interviewer may ask a receptionist or other employee in the waiting area who has observed you waiting for their opinion of you. For this reason you must recognize that you are 'on stage' even in the waiting area.

The do's and don'ts of waiting in the reception area

- Do sit in a relaxed but slightly formal way.
- Don't read magazines or newspapers to pass the time.
- Do review your prepared questions and interview notes.
- Do rehearse in your mind the Five steps to self-selling.

An interviewer may or may not shake hands when they meet you in the waiting area. Follow their cue and only shake hands if they offer theirs. Often an interviewer will offer you a cup of tea or coffee. This is a polite and welcoming gesture on their part

23

Do not accept tea or coffee – it could weaken your position and you could spill it!

A polite refusal would sound something like this: 'No, thank you, I had a cup just before I arrived.' From a professional standpoint, accepting coffee weakens your negotiating position at the first interview. The subliminal message is that you are being casual, familiar and on a social call. Professionals do not want to communicate this message. Professionals want to communicate stability and a focused business attitude. Also, I have heard stories from human resource personnel and other managers who have actually had applicants spill their drink all over themselves and the desk. More than likely, you will have some stage fright, so don't create more chances for you to trip up! However, it is perfectly acceptable to take coffee at the final interview after an offer has been made and you're more relaxed. This gesture denotes, on a subliminal level, that you integrate easily and are a welcomed new member to the team.

══ 24 ══

At the first interview, do not discuss what the exact salary would be — leave the subject open and discuss such details after an offer has been made (probably at the final interview)

In most circumstances, you should not discuss salary at the first interview. The interviewer will make a point of asking you your salary requirements. If it is the first interview, always respond, 'Not fixed'. Countless individuals have lost job opportunities by answering this question by giving an exact amount.

The odds are that, if you state a figure that is too high, you will appear demanding and overrated. Conversely, if you state a figure that is too low, you'll be perceived as a poor performer.

After you state that your salary requirements are not fixed, explain to the interviewer that you have come to the interview with an open mind. Explain further that you believe that the right position with the right benefits would make the salary an issue about which you could be flexible.

Don't make the mistake of going to the first interview and making salary/compensation demands. It shouldn't even be discussed. It is assumed that you would not have gone to the interview if you did not feel that the position would at least be likely to offer you the sort of salary you require. Discussion of salary and compensation requirements come at the final interview, after a job offer has been made. At this point, it has been determined that they want you. What a great feeling it is to be wanted! Now you are in a better position to negotiate.

What if they state some kind of objection during an interview? A typical one may be stated as, 'You seem like you don't have enough experience', or 'We were looking for someone with a bit more diversity of experience in their background'. What should you do? The first thing to do is relax. See objections as a positive experience. Rejoice when you hear an objection. It means that the interviewer is thinking and trying to give you full consideration.

I would be wary of any interviewer who does not have any objections. If they have no objections, it more than likely means they are not interested in you at all.

Four ways in which to handle an objection

There are four times at which it is appropriate to handle an objection in an interview.

1 Before they ask

The night before the interview, you should make a list of the most obvious objections that might come up in the interview. Be ready for the obvious and even bring it up before they ask. For example, if you truly don't have years of experience and you know it's going to come up, attack it head on. They will respect you for it. Say, 'I know I don't have five to ten years' experience like some, but I do have an open-minded will-try-anything attitude. I don't stop working until I achieve satisfactory results.'

2 When they ask

Again, preparation ahead of time in your role plays will help you come across as confident and smooth. You can really impress the interviewer by sounding like you welcome adversity. After all, problem-solving is a respected quality in business professionals. Once the objection has been stated, you respond with, 'I'm glad you asked that' or 'That's a good question'. Then proceed to give your explanation.

3 Later

It may not be appropriate in your mind to handle the objection as soon as it is raised. The interviewer will understand, as long as you have a good reason for putting off an answer. For instance, the objection could be, 'I don't think we have the budget available to hire someone at your level of experience. You appear to be overqualified.' You could respond with, 'The important thing is that you feel comfortable with my abilities. We can discuss salary later.

I'm sure we can work out something that is mutually agreeable.'

4 Never

This situation in objection-handling is rare, but it is appropriate in certain instances. Usually, it works best with objections that are minor, such as, 'It sounds like you are qualified; however, it would be even better if you knew how to operate X instead of Y.' You then intentionally dust the objection under the carpet so as not to make a mountain out of a molehill. Simply continue to sell yourself and draw attention to the fact that X and Y are quite similar and so there is no reason to split hairs over this type of issue.

Practise! Practise! Practise! Come home from an interview and write down the objections you may have mishandled, or a question you know you did not have a reasonable answer to. Then practise handling the objections with well-thought-out, prepared answers in a mirror or with a friend.

The worst thing to do when hearing an objection is to argue. Take, for instance, the objection, 'You appear to be overqualified and out of our salary range.' A person easily could become indignant and say, 'You're a big company. You should be able to afford quality when you find it.' That would lose you the job. Don't argue about anything in an interview. The interviewer is always right. One company I worked for purposely instructed interviewers to create objections and to cause friction at interviews. You can take issue with anything you want. However, you might win the battle but lose the war.

Here is a simple but effective four-step method to handling objections. You can remember it by memorizing *LAER*. *L* stands for *Listen*. Leaning forward when you hear an objection and keeping eye contact demonstrates you are confident and would make a good employee. *A* stands for *Acknowledge*. Repeat back in paraphrase form the objection you just heard. This tells the interviewer you were listening and that you understand the question. It also clarifies the question. It would be embarrassing to have misunderstood the question. *E* stands for *Explore*. Ask an open question, such as, 'Tell me more about why you feel that way' or 'Why do you ask that?' The explore stage helps you to gather more information about their objection. Always remember in any negotiations that the more information you have, the more power you have. Finally, R stands for *Respond*. You now have completed enough preliminaries to respond effectively. Unfortunately, many individuals go right from objection to respond, missing out all the middle steps. Can you see how much more effective you can be when you include all the other steps?

In summary, the interview is a selling situation. The one who sells the best, wins. Remember, you are the greatest product you will ever sell.

Let's review what we've learned in this chapter.

- Before the interview, prepare – compile a list of questions you will ask the recruiter;
- Role play the interview with a friend, following the five steps to self-selling and rehearse the questions you will ask the interviewer as well as the questions you are likely to be asked;
- Arrive at the interview 15 minutes early;
- Be professional as you wait in the waiting area;
- Do not accept tea or coffee at an interview;
- Do not discuss salary at the first interview.

6
Follow up effectively

On arriving home after your interview, feeling a bit relieved and elated that it's all over, you still have work to do. Work that, when performed properly, will keep your name ahead of the competition long after the interview has passed. In following up an interview, you're on the home stretch to getting a job in 30 days. Effective follow-up requires a delicate, tactful technique. Begin with sending a thank you note.

===== 25 =====

Send a handwritten thank you note to the interviewer, thanking them for the interview and enclosing any further information that may aid your application

After each interview, send a handwritten thank you note to the interviewer. It is appropriate to send a computer-generated letter if you wish. However, you have already sent your CV and covering letter to them, which were printed off using a computer, and that was a hi-tech presentation. Writing a thank you note by hand adds the human touch, some personal warmth. Also, it indicates sincerity and attention to detail, so it's another chance to sell some of your good qualities.

A sample thank you letter

A good thank you letter should contain the following elements. It should:

- thank the interviewer for the interview;
- reconfirm your interest in the position;
- confirm your understanding of the next step;
- enclose any new information or developments that may help you get the job;.
- if necessary, nudge the employer into a decision by indicating that another employer is very interested and another job offer is imminent.

Sample thank you letter

Name   Date
House name/number Street
City/Town/Village
County and postcode

Dear Mr/Ms _____,
Re: (Job applying for)

Thank you for the interview - I enjoyed meeting you.

On leaving your office, I had time to reflect on our discussion about organising schedules visually so that they are clear, easy to understand and can be updated quickly. I am therefore sending you, under separate cover, copies on disk of the schedule formats I have designed that we discussed at the interview. I hope this proves useful to you.

I recall you mentioning that you will be discussing all the applicants' interviews with the department manager before deciding who to offer the job to. I was wondering when you will be able to let me know your decision, as another employer has expressed an interest.

However, I was most impressed when I came on (day) and do sincerely hope you will choose me. My phone number is _____.

I shall look forward to hearing from you.

Yours sincerely,

(Your name)

An alternative is to call the interviewer once or twice after the interview. Don't be horrified by the thought of doing this, just don't be intrusive!

═══ 26 ═══

Call the interviewer once or twice after the interview – if you sense a high level of interest after the first call, call again

Following up can work in your favour if you use this simple formula. First, give a valid reason for making the follow-up call. The worst thing you can do is to call and ask, 'How are things going with my job application?' It is better to say, 'I am calling to see if, having gone through my application form and interview notes, there is any additional information you might need.' Thank them for their time and ask when they anticipate reaching a decision and how they will let you know.

The main purpose of this type of follow-up is to take what I call 'a temperature check'. If they appear to be cold and indifferent, go on to other priorities. If they appear to be warm and enthusiastic, consider it a likely prospect and plan other forms of follow-up until you get a job offer. A tactic I have used successfully for my likely prospects is to call by their office a week or two after the interview. This tactic may sound pushy to you, but it really isn't as long as it's done properly. If they are at all interested in you, they will respect you for making the effort.

Before ringing to follow up, check your telephone skills. Always smile when you are speaking on the telephone – it does come across to the person you are speaking to.. Many large telephone operations such as airline reservation rooms require mirrors in front of the operators. Smiling makes your voice sound like you are an energetic and responsible person.

Now you're ready to call, here's how to do it. Telephone the interviewer and state that tomorrow you will be in the vicinity and would like to stop by for a moment. Explain you have some new references or copies of previous projects you have worked on that you would like to share with them to add to your application. If they are at all interested in you, they will welcome this new information. Just make sure you have substantial, new information to bring. That's why, when at all possible, you should hold a few things back from the interview so you can use them later as a reason to visit and follow up.

Arrive at their office at the designated time and be sure you have with you exactly what you promised to bring. At the end of your time together, close by asking about the job. If it is not offered, think about your next step in the hiring process.

I went for an interview with one manager many years ago and then used this tactic three times. It worked! I was determined to get the job and, over a period of two months, I visited his office three times and asked about the job at the end of each session. At the second session, he invited his boss in to meet me. They both asked in unison before showing me the door, 'Do you have any further questions?' 'Yes,' I replied politely, 'when do I start?' I must admit, I noticed shock in their eyes. It appeared that it was the last question they expected! They both grinned and said, 'We'll see, let's stay in touch.' I may not have received a job offer that very day, but I do believe that my ability to remain persistent and ask about the job – directly in the last instance – earned me an offer a few days later.

27

Love the word 'no' – learn to love rejection, as the more 'no' responses you get, the closer you are to a 'yes' and you only need one yes!

As suggested in Chapter 4, we should learn to love the word 'no'. We should also, as mentioned, make a commitment to accelerate the number of 'no' responses we are going to get. The reason, you realize, is that for every 'no' we get, we are one step closer to a 'yes'. Always remember the illustration of the casino and numbers game. All you need is one 'yes'! The odds are in your favour.

How far do you go in following up? Is there a point when you should just simply move on? In answer to these questions, I'll share a short true story and you can draw your own conclusion. A few years ago, I responded to a job ad in a newspaper. A few weeks later, I received the standard rejection letter. You know the one, 'I am sorry, although we were very impressed with your qualifications, another applicant had a more suitable background for the position', etc. etc. Now, most people would normally take that kind of letter as a bald statement of fact, file it in the bin and move on. I didn't. I was not going to take 'no' for an answer. My own self-talk was, 'I want to work for you, and you're going to give me a job.' I immediately drafted a letter to the Human Resources Manager. First, I thanked the Manager for writing to me regarding my application. Next, I went back to selling myself. I wrote down some ideas based on my CV as to where I might fit into their company. Then, I closed for action by saying, 'I would be grateful if you would meet with me to discuss possibilities further.' I enclosed an expanded three-page version of the one-page CV I had sent them when I had originally responded to their advert. Within a week of posting the letter, I was contacted by the Manager's assistant. I went for a job interview that same week and within a month I was employed at their head office with my own office. When do you stop following up? You be the judge.

Be forewarned not to carry on selling yourself after a job offer has been made. Learn to stop talking! You could talk yourself out of a job. Instead, at this point, focus your energy on negotiating your salary, benefits, and when you will start.

28

When a job offer comes, stop selling yourself!

This is a perfect time to say that it is in your best interest to initially accept all positions offered to you. Always say 'yes', even if the terms are not totally agreeable to you. The place to make your final decision, though, is at home with your family and when you have had time to mull it over in your own mind. If, after thinking about it, you do not want the position, you can always call and decline or even ask to renegotiate terms. If they want you badly enough, they will negotiate.

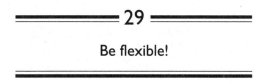

29

Be flexible!

Being flexible once a job offer has been made is very important. The ideal situation may not exist. A job that initially has a lower income than you would like may have great potential for promotion, good experience and so on, and this may be the best way to get your foot in the door. With a good company, you are embarking on the start of a solid career. Remember, in such cases, what appears to be short-term loss actually has long-term gain.

Accepting an Offer

After you have received an offer and said that you will accept it, you should write to confirm this. Send your letter after you have received the company's letter offering you the job. Your acceptance letter is not a legal contract, but sets out what the job is as you understand it. Mention in the letter such things as the date and time of a medical examination (if required), the first day of work, what the job is, what your title will be, who you will be reporting to and what your salary and other benefits will be.

Sample job acceptance letter

```
                                    Name
                      House name/number
                                  Street
                      City/town/village
                      County and postcode


Date


Name
Title
Company
Street
City/town/village
County and postcode


Dear Mr/Ms _____

Re: (Job applying for)

I am pleased to accept your offer of the
position of (job title) for (company) at the
monthly salary of (£_____). I shall be
reporting to (manager's name). I understand,
too, that I am to have a medical examination
on (day, date, time) at (company name and
location).

As requested in your letter, I shall report
to your office at 9.00 on (date). I look
forward to joining (company) and will always
endeavour to work hard and cause you to be
happy you decided on me.

Thank you for this opportunity to be a member
of your team.

Yours sincerely,
(Handwritten signature)


(Your name, typed)
```

Rejecting an offer

As you have been very actively searching for a job for 30 days, it is more than likely you will have received more than one job offer. As soon as you have made a decision that you would like to work for a particular company, notify all the other employers you have received offers from of your decision. In your letter, thank them for their interest, explain that it was a difficult decision to make but that another opportunity proved a better fit with your current interests and requirements. Don't burn any bridges, though: say this in a way that implies that you might well contact them in the future – you may need to. It is not necessary to give the name of the company you have ultimately chosen to work for.

Sample job offer rejection letter

Name
House name/number
Street
City/town/village
County and postcode

Date

Name
Title
Company
Street
City/town/village
County and postcode

Dear Mr/Ms

Re: (job applying for)

Thank you for offering me the position of
(job title) with (company). I have just
accepted a similar position with another
company and so I am afraid I cannot accept
your offer.

This has been a difficult decision to make
as I was very impressed by your company and
enjoyed meeting you when I came for
interview. However, I look forward to the
possibility of our paths crossing again in
the future.

Yours sincerely,
(Handwritten signature)

(Your name, typed)

═══ 30 ═══

There is no such thing as good luck
– rely totally on a good plan and
good selling, as set out here, and
you will achieve your goal

The next chapter sets out a 30-day activity planner, which has been designed to help you put into practice the proven system described so far. The daily activities monitored in this planner are what will make you successful in your search for a job. They create the very difference that will make your job hunting more successful and a more positive experience this time than in the past.

Faithfully perform the activities set out in this plan and fill in the relevant details for the next 30 days. Commit yourself to the work described in the plan; be relentless and determined to achieve your goal. With your determination and this plan, you will definitely come out a winner. In fact, you are a winner now if you believe it.

Let's review what we have learned in this chapter.

- Send a thank you note.
- Call the interviewer once or twice after the interview, but have a reason for calling.
- Remember, the more 'no' responses you get, the closer you are to a 'yes'.
- Learn when to stop selling yourself.
- Be flexible.
- Do not rely on luck – rely on the activity planner, described next.

7
The activity planner

Why use an Activity Planner? Isn't it enough to read this book? The answer is 'no'. Information that is not put into action remains simply that, information. The activity planner is what makes this job search system effective. It is the only book of its kind that allows you to monitor key job hunting activities on a daily basis. This book and the activity planner are the only job hunting tools you will ever need.

The activity planner provides you with a concise synopsis of the entire book. You will notice that each day features a corresponding key concept. And, during the 30 days, you will discover new ways to refine the key concepts and tailor them to your needs. Again, you will become aware of the main ideas as you see them listed on a daily basis.

To create your activity planner, take an exercise book or a file of 30 A4 pages. Taking the key concepts in chronological order, write one at the top of each page. This action plan provides you with two attack options. The first is to work diligently every day of the week, except the weekends, for 30 days. The second is to work non-stop every day of the week for 30 days. The first option provides you, at the end of 30 days, with 120 contacts. However, for those of you with the time, to assure even greater success, I recommend that you pursue the second option. That way, you will create a total of 180 leads. Should you decide on this latter option, fill in the pages marked 'Bonus Days', to represent the weekends. The difference between 120 and 180 could mean having or not having more than one offer to choose from. Commit yourself to the extra work if you can afford the time.

This action plan also requires that you register your CV with as many of the Internet's online CV databases as possible, as explained in Chapter 4. Also, that you take the time to search online employer databases and send them your electronic CV. The electronic job search is a required bonus activity as then you can diversify your job search and it works as extra insurance for getting a job offer within 30 days. However important these activities are, they do not replace the day-to-day activities using conventional means that are also outlined in this plan.

Be aware that 'Day one' stands for a Monday. Begin your action plan on a Monday, when you are fresh and a new working week has begun. Also, this will ensure the 'Bonus days' fall on weekends, should you decide to increase the quantity and quality of your job hunting work.

The activity planner is a step-by-step action plan that, when diligently followed, will get you a job in 30 days or in even less time. Follow the steps listed here closely and complete the activity planner from beginning to end. The activity planner must be completed on a daily basis if you are to put the proper amount of work into your search for a job and for your strategy to be effective. Remember, do not rely on good luck. Rather, rely on a good plan – the activity planner.

Week 1

DAY 1
If you think you can't, you won't, but if you think you can, you will!

DAY 2
Practise positive self-talk: 'I can, I will! I know I can do it!'

DAY 3
Neutralize negative self-talk ('I'll never find a good job') with positive, winning statements

DAY 4
Don't blame others – take responsibility for yourself and your career

DAY 5
Practise visualization when you are lying awake in the morning or evening, seeing yourself already working at and enjoying the career you want

BONUS DAY 6
Dress like a winner

Week 2

BONUS DAY 7
Design a one-page CV, giving just enough information to prompt an interview – leave the reader wanting more

DAY 8
Print out your CV on white paper only, using a professional computer software CV template, use the spell check facility and make sure that your grammar is correct

DAY 9
Use action words constantly throughout your CV. Take the time to be creative and use a thesaurus to avoid duplication

DAY 10
Target your CV to each particular company you write to and each position you apply for

DAY 11
An effective covering letter is divided into three distinct paragraphs, each with its own purpose: attention; benefit; close for action.

DAY 12
The purpose of the CV and covering letter is to get you the interview

BONUS DAY 13
Secure six new leads a day (30 a week) and send them a covering letter and your CV. (See days 14, 15 and 16 for where to find new leads.)

BONUS DAY 14
Secure ten leads a week from newspapers' recruitment sections, sending a covering letter and your CV

Week 3

DAY 15
Secure ten leads a week from making cold calls

DAY 16
Secure five leads per week from the Yellow Pages, the phone book or a business directory

DAY 17
Secure five leads by networking –
attend all relevant business
association meetings and community
organizations' functions

DAY 18
Develop sources of leads relentlessly,
including use of the Internet (do this
daily from 9.00 until 5.00 or, if you
are working, in the evenings and at
weekends) until you achieve your
goal

DAY 19
At an interview, there are two ways to
learn about the company: by listening
and by asking good questions

BONUS DAY 20
Role play to rehearse for the interview

Week 4

BONUS DAY 21
Arrive for the interview 15 minutes early, do not arrive late or on time

DAY 22
While filling out pre-interview forms, sit in a relaxed but slightly formal way and, rather than read magazines in the waiting area, read the notes you've been using to prepare yourself for the interview

DAY 23
Do not accept tea or coffee at an interview as it could weaken your position and you could spill it!

DAY 24
At the first interview, do not discuss what the exact salary would be – leave the subject open and discuss such details after an offer has been made (probably at the final interview)

DAY 25
Send a handwritten thank you note to the interviewer, thanking them for the interview and enclosing any further information that may aid your application

DAY 26
Call the interviewer once or twice after the interview – if you sense a high level of interest after the first call, call again

BONUS DAY 27
Love the word 'no' – learn to love rejection, as the more 'no' responses you get, the closer you are to a 'yes' and you only need one yes!

BONUS DAY 28
When a job offer comes, stop selling yourself!

Week 5

DAY 29
Be flexible! A position with a lower salary, but great potential, is often the best way to get your foot in the door. What seems to be short-term loss could actually create long-term gains

DAY 30
Rely on this book's activity planner. There is no such thing as good luck. Rely totally on a good plan and good selling, as set out here, and you will achieve your goal

8
Progress checker

CHECK ATTITUDE

Today I used positive self-talk and visualization and I was:

- in a positive frame of mind all day ☐
- positive for only part of the day ☐
- doubtful and negative most of the day ☐

CHECK LEAD GENERATION

I discovered six new likely leads today (list them below).

	Company Name	Contact
1		
2		
3		
4		
5		
6		

CHECK COVERING LETTER AND CV

I sent covering letters and CVs to all six new likely leads (list below).

	Company name	Contact	Address	Phone number
1				
2				
3				
4				
5				
6				

CHECK INTERVIEW TECHNIQUE

I practised interviewing by role playing situations with a friend (list interviews).

	Company name	Contact	Date/ Time	Address	Phone number
1					
2					
3					

CHECK THANK YOU NOTES SENT

Thank you notes sent? Yes_____ No_____

	Company name	Contact	Address	Phone number
1				
2				
3				

CHECK FOLLOW-UP PHONE CALLS MADE

Follow-up phone calls made? Yes_____ No_____

	Company name	Contact	Address	Phone number
1				
2				
3				

CHECK CV REGISTERED ON THE INTERNET

Today, I registered my CV with at least one online CV service.

	Service's name	Internet address	Other information
1			
2			
3			

CHECK EMPLOYER DATABASES ON THE INTERNET

Today, I searched employer databases and sent at least three electronic CVs or profiles to prospective employers.

	Company Name	Internet address	Other information
1			
2			
3			

Bibliography

Elsea, Janet G (1984) *The Four-minute Sell*, Simon & Schuster, New York.

Grappo, Gary Joseph (1996) *The Top 10 Fears of Job Seekers*, Berkley Books, New York.

Grappo, Gary Joseph (1994) *How to Write Better Resumes,* Barron's, New York.

Grappo, Gary Joseph (1997) *The Top Ten Career Strategies for Making a Living in the 21st Century*, Berkley Books, New York.

Helmstetter, Dr Shad (1986) *What to Say When You Talk to Yourself*, Simon & Schuster, New York.

Jackson, Tom (1978) *Guerrilla Tactics in the Job Market*, Bantam Books, New York.

Sinetar, Marsha (1989) *Do What You Love, the Money Will Follow*. Dell, New York.

Tracy, Brian (1990) *The Science of Self-confidence* (tape series), Solana Beach, California.

Tracy, Brian (1990) *The Psychology of Success*, (tape series), Solana Beach, California.

Waitley, Dr Denis (1986) *The Psychology of Winning*, Berkley Books, New York.

Further Reading from Kogan Page

A–Z of Careers and Jobs, 8th edn, Diane Burston
Creating Your Career, Simon Kent
Great Answers to Tough Interview Questions: How to Get the Job You Want, 3rd edn, Martin and John Yate
How to Pass Graduate Recruitment Tests, Mike Bryon
How to Pass Numeracy Tests, Harry Toley and Ken Thomas
How to Pass Selection Tests, Mike Bryon and Sanjay Modha
How to Pass Technical Selection Tests, Mike Bryon and Sanjay Modha
How to Pass the Civil Service Qualifying Tests, Mike Bryon
How to Pass Verbal Reasoning Tests, Harry Tolley and Ken Thomas
How You Can Get That Job! Application Forms and Letters Made Easy, Rebecca Corfield
The Job Hunter's Handbook, David Greenwood
Job Hunting after University or College, Jan Perrett
Job Hunting Made Easy: A Step-by-Step Guide, 3rd edn, John Bramham and David Cox
Manage Your Own Career, Ben Bell
Offbeat Careers: 60 Ways to Avoid Becoming an Accountant, 3rd edn, Vivien Donald
Preparing Your Own CV, Rebecca Corfield
Readymade Job Search Letters, Lynn Williams
Test Your Own Aptitude, 2nd edn, Jim Barrett and Geoff Williams
Working Abroad: The Daily Telegraph Guide to Working and Living Overseas, 19th edn, Godfrey Golzen
Working for Yourself: The Daily Telegraph Guide to Self-Employment, 17th edn, Godfrey Golzen
Your First Job, 3rd edn, Vivien Donald and Ray Grose

The Kogan Page Careers in... Series:
Accountancy *(6th edition)*
Architecture *(5th edition)*
Art and Design *(8th edition)*
Banking and Finance *(4th edition)*
Catering, Hotel Administration and Management *(5th edition)*

Computing and Information Technology *(1st edition)*
Environmental Conservation *(6th edition)*
Fashion *(5th edition)*
Film and Video *(5th edition)*
Hairdressing and Beauty Therapy *(7th edition)*
Journalism *(8th edition)*
The Law *(8th edition)*
Marketing, Advertising and Public Relations *(6th edition)*
Medicine, Dentistry and Mental Health *(7th edition)*
Nursing and Related Professions *(7th edition)*
Police Force *(5th edition)*
Publishing and Bookselling *(2nd edition)*
Retailing *(6th edition)*
Secretarial and Office Work *(7th edition)*
Social Work *(6th edition)*
Sport *(6th edition)*
Teaching *(7th edition)*
Television and Radio *(7th edition)*
The Theatre *(6th edition)*
Travel Industry *(6th edition)*
Using English *(1st edition)*
Using Languages *(8th edition)*
Working Outdoors *(7th edition)*
Working with Animals *(8th edition)*
Working with Children and Young People *(7th edition)*

Correspond with the author
directly on the Internet

Mr Grappo appreciates hearing from readers of his books and those who have come to his seminars. Write when you have an experience to share as a result of reading and responding to something in one of his books. Success stories based on putting his concepts into practice are always welcome. Contact him on: *gjgjoseph@aol.com*

Index